A MINDFUL KITCHEN
COOKING WITH THE SIX PERFECTIONS

PADMA YVONNE JAQUES

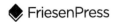
FriesenPress

Suite 300 - 990 Fort St
Victoria, BC, Canada, V8V 3K2
www.friesenpress.com

Copyright © 2016 by Padma Yvonne Jaques
First Edition — 2016

Author: Padma Yvonne Jaques

Contributors: Floriana Albi, John Buchanan, Christine Buchanan, Hilary Cole, Jordan Commandeur, Michelle Dumond, Leonarda Ehl, Sarah Enright - Thrive Graphic Design, Karen Husak, Muzzy Jaques, Roger Jaques, Sherri Kajiwara, Yuliya Kam'yanska, Joni Leung, Mariska McLean, Lada Paul, Miriam Plishka, Deedee Poyner, Hilde Wagner

Diamond Forest Photography: Padma Yvonne, Roger Jaques
Editor: Jeffrey Bryan, Akira Communications
Food Photography: Albert Yee Loy
Foodstyling: Sherri Kajiwara
Gabriola Photography: Nicholas Halpin
Page 40 Photography: Larry Scherban
Photographs on pages 66 - 74: Free online sources
Translations of Master Shantideva's Guide to the
Bodhisattva's Way of Life: Geshe Michael Roach

ISBN
978-1-4602-7383-8 (Hardcover)
978-1-4602-7384-5 (Paperback)
978-1-4602-7385-2 (eBook)

1. Cooking, Courses & Dishes

Distributed to the trade by The Ingram Book Company

CONTENTS

Diamond Forest Rainbow Salad

Charred Peppers and Mushroom Salad

Massaged Kale Toss with Beets and Oranges

Float Point Salad

Lali's Root Roast with Goat Cheese

Broccoli Timbales

Nutty Green Beans

Lemony Beets

Cabbage Sauté

Mama Hilde's Sweet and Sour Red Cabbage (with a Twist)

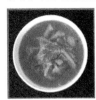
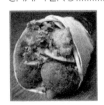

DEDICATION

WE DEDICATE THIS COOKBOOK TO ALL OUR PERFECT teachers—our dear mothers, our heart guru Geshe Michael Roach, Lama Christie McNally, our children, Swami Muktibodhananda Saraswati, Swami Satyananda Saraswati who is always with us in spirit, our food guru Sally Fallon, Dr. Weston Price, our many teachers from the Ayurvedic tradition and to Sherri, who asked for it! Thank you to the Diamond Bodied Piglets (DBPs as we affectionately called our direct retreat caretakers) and to their countless emanations for keeping us in retreat.

As our deep retreat came to a close in the autumn of 2013 we pondered what we would find 'out there' and how it would look to us. We experienced, over and over, washes of immense gratitude. How on earth did we get to do this? How is it that we spent close to three years in silent, deep isolation? How did it come to be that we had an ideal retreat cabin on a perfect piece of quiet, secluded land at the highest point of a tiny Pacific Northwest island—7 kilometres wide by 18 kilometres long? Why did SPUD (Sustainable Produce Urban Delivery - www.spud.ca) just happen to service this tiny island? They deliver organic produce and groceries in Vancouver, Victoria, Toronto... and Gabriola Island! At least for the entire duration of our retreat! How did that work? And where did the remote 707-acre designated park five minutes from our cabin come from? There was rarely another

person in there when we went for our decompression walks. What celestial providence sent us our families, friends, and our devoted DBPs and their limitless emanations? And how did we ever find our precious teachers? Without them we would have nothing—no deep retreat, no cookbook. They taught us everything. They sourced and translated the ancient texts from Sanskrit and Tibetan into not only English, but other-worldly English. We first heard about the Six Perfections from our heart guru Geshe Michael after he had long since translated the root texts and written divinely inspired commentaries on them. We thank you from the deepest, very centre of our hearts.

Padma Yvonne & Roger Jaques
Diamond Forest Retreat Centre
Gabriola, BC Canada , 2014

INTRODUCTION

RECIPES FROM DEEP RETREAT:
COOKING WITH HOT OIL

ON DECEMBER 30, 2010, WE CLOSED THE gates to our five-acre retreat property on Gabriola Island, BC, Canada. Our intent? To do a silent, isolated meditation and yoga retreat for three years. For seven years, we had been studying hard with our primary teachers in the Dalai Lama's lineage of Tibetan Buddhism and in the yogic science lineage of the *Hatha Yoga Pradipika*. It was our goal to practice what our teachers had taught us. We had been rigorously trained to do a Great Retreat, but you can never really be ready for what it's like and what happens in such an isolated and contained environment. We were in retreat for just under three years—a very long time to be in silent isolation from the world.

While the title of this introduction might be *Cooking with Hot Oil*, this is not a book about deep frying! I wrote this while we were in deep retreat and attempting to be Bodhisattvas, whose career path is practicing the Six Perfections. Bodhisattvas are always cooking with hot oil in the sense of upping the ante on their spiritual practice, getting the most bang for their buck, raising the bar, and trying to

PADMA YVONNE JAQUES

make the most of their lives and opportunities with the ultimate goal of reaching enlightenment for the sake of every single living being. They do this through continuously living these six precepts of perfection.

In 2012 our spiritual teacher and retreat advisor, Geshe Michael Roach, gave us a priceless piece of advice. He said that if we were experiencing what the Christian mystics call *aridity* in our spiritual practice, a good way to infuse some juice into our meditations was to serve others by joining the caretaking team for a short time. We took this advice to heart.

Without breaking our own deep retreat, we asked our close students and caretakers to allow us

the opportunity to caretake them in a much, much smaller way than they were caretaking us. We asked that they permit us to prepare and serve them their main meal of the day during the retreats they did here at Diamond Forest Retreat Centre. Some of them kept asking for the recipes of the meals we sent them, however I rarely cook from a recipe! By the time they asked, I had usually forgotten exactly how I made any particular dish. I was faced with this conundrum when Sherri Kajiwara—who was heading up our caretaking team on the outside—was doing a five-week retreat in our yurt, and suggested I write a cookbook!

For these recipes I was inspired by the foods I watched our mothers make, tasted at restaurants, learned from friends or adapted from someone else's cookbook. I tended to make dishes up or modify them depending on what we had left over, what we had in the garden, what SPUD brought us in our weekly bin, and whatever we happened to be craving.

Of course, all that changed when Sherri asked us to write this cookbook to raise money for the Vancouver dharma centre called Three Jewels Vancouver and for a deep-retreat centre in B.C. that would serve the needs of future long-term retreat groups.

I realized I would have to make a commitment to finding consistency in our meals. I would have to ascertain the exact proportions, cooking times, and temperatures. In other words, I would have to determine the precise cause of a certain desired result.

It's exactly the same with aspiring Bodhisattvas. First of all, they experience a burning desire, an obsession really, to find the true and consistently lasting causes of love, happiness, joy, and the foolproof method of eliminating suffering. Then they realize that every single being alive, not just the human ones, are hell bent on exactly these same deep-seated needs. So they make a commitment to finding consistent dependability in exactly how to bring about these results.

In the case of a Bodhisattva, these causes are the Six Perfections, and the result is enlightenment for ourselves and for all.

It is this wish which allows a limitless
Mass of living beings to attain
The highest form of happiness, with ease.

Those who hope to smash the thousand pains
Of the cycle of life, or to solve
The unhappiness of every living being,
Or bring them to the many thousand forms
Of happiness, must never give up
This very wish for enlightenment

Master Shantideva, *Guide to the Bodhisattva's Way of Life*

It is the burning desire of the Bodhisattva that is like a special seed. This seed ripens into the highest form of happiness for all beings, simply through the practice of the Six Perfections, without the need to "undertake any such difficult practices as undertaking the life of a cave-dwelling yogi," (Gyaltsab Je Dharma Rinchen, *Commentary to the Guide to the Bodhisattva's Way of Life*).

So just in case spending three years in silence in isolated retreat isn't on your agenda, don't worry. All you need is the wish. All you need is the burning desire. All you need is love.

It struck us like a bolt of lightning! There is no such thing as the exact cause of a certain desired result when you're talking about cooking. In fact, even the most precise recipe in the most technical cookbook can fail dismally due to operator error or perhaps it just doesn't agree with your palate.

In fact, the same food (or medicine or book or musical genre) can be one person's panacea or paradise and another person's poison or nightmare! Have you noticed? It's like escargots (snails), which my mother adores and finds truly delectable. We'll leave it to you to guess how I feel about them! Or horror movies which we absolutely refused to watch, while others find them highly amusing and entertaining. So which is it? Are snails delicious or despicable? Are horror movies hilarious or horrendous? Is it heavy metal or is it heavy opera that is God's gift to all music lovers?

You could say both, or you could say neither. And you would be right either way, wouldn't you? It's because those qualities of snails or horror movies or musical genres don't exist *in* them. Rather, they're being applied *to* them by the viewer, taster, experiencer. But what if those *applied* qualities change? So one day I decide to try escargots just one more time, and *wow*, I find them scrumptious. It could happen! People who used to be our worst enemies are now our closest friends, and vice versa. We develop a taste for opera and lose our obsession with heavy metal. Roger used to hate cilantro but now, you will find it in many of the recipes. It works like that, doesn't it?

We call this emptiness, or you could also call it infinite potential. The potential of food or medicine to nourish or heal doesn't actually arise from within them because any effects are not what science would call reproducible—consistent every single time, for every single person. That's what we call being empty of having such a fixed, unchanging nature or set of qualities.

Eventually, it becomes clear that it's not only other people, places, foods, movies, books, interactions, etc., that don't have a specific self-nature of being any particular way or having a set of qualities inherent within them. We, as individuals, don't even have a specific set of qualities that we can call "me", which are constant across time, which are agreed on by all, always. How do we know this? Because it depends on who's looking! If those qualities were coming *from* me or the food or the medicine, then *everyone* experiencing or looking would have to be seeing or experiencing the same thing. Well, if they're not coming *from* me or the food or the medicine, where are they coming from? We want our medicine to cure our migraine, or our spiritual practice to turn us into a realized being, or food to nourish our bodies! How on earth do we ever create a result if we can't seem to pinpoint the cause? Where is the consistent dependability? How do we create a cookbook that nourishes, or a world of bliss for all?

Sally Fallon says in *Nourishing Traditions*,

To make us healthy, our food must taste good, it must be digestible, and it must be eaten in peace. Even whole foods, properly prepared according to traditional methods, do us no good if we eat them with a grudge; they will not confer health on the man [or woman] who does not forgive.

It isn't the medicine that is the cure; rather, it depends on whether we have within us the seed potential for the medicine to cure us. How do we plant this seed potential? We do so through a conscious effort to help cure others when they are in pain or sick.

It isn't the music that creates the bliss. It depends on whether our own seeds for ecstasy are ripening within us through having had the wish to make others happy through musical or other creative endeavours.

It isn't the escargots that contain and exude deliciousness! It's whether or not we have served others many meals that we took great pains to prepare and make delicious.

Let's extrapolate a little more. Qualities we see in others, like our partners, do not come from them either. So is it staying with our current partner or finding another partner that will make us happy when the relationship reaches its seemingly inevitable speed bumps? It's neither. It depends on what kind of seeds we have planted—ones that will either ripen as future happiness for us or not.

The same thing applies to a job. Should one quit this over or under demanding job and find another? Have you noticed how these themes seem to take on a patterned refrain? How many jobs have we quit and started? How many relationships have we quit and started? Did it work? Could it be that the cause for satisfaction and happiness in occupations and relationships doesn't come from the job or the partner? Our teacher says, and so does Master Shantideva, just take care of others. It's a catch-all phrase, but it actually does work. The seeds we plant when we take care of others always ripen as an experience of us being cared for—whether that manifests as a loving partner, a satisfying job, nourishing food, medication that heals, music that thrills, and so forth. So if it's not the qualities within the food that nourish us, why would we concern ourselves with organic vs. non-organic, raw milk vs. pasteurized, unrefined vs. highly refined salt?

Like the medicine and the job or the socks that warm our feet, these things still work! Medicine *functions*, there's no doubt about it. Check the revenue statements of the drug companies! The job works—we are productively engaged. The socks that my mother knit us certainly worked! That's why we wore them. But it could only be because we have kept someone warm. That's WHY they worked.

PADMA YVONNE JAQUES

How Food Works

We accept the truths as being two:
The one which is deceptive [HOW it works],
And the one which is the ultimate [WHY it works].
Master Shantideva, *Guide to the Bodhisattva's Way of Life*

The consistently dependable cause of *why* something works has to come first because we need to have planted the seeds to experience things the way we would like. Then the causes and conditions, or *how* it works, arise to ripen our seeds. Then for example, organic produce *will* taste way better, and fresh eggs from humanely treated, free-roaming chickens *will* increase our body's ability to absorb vitamins.

Don't take anything I say for granted. These are ideas that need to be tried and tested in the laboratory of your own life. It's not until we have thought about these ideas extensively and experimented with them that their power to transform emerges. They have within them the firepower to annihilate all the seeds we may have planted previously for pain and suffering.

When we use these concepts consciously as a way to re-think our negative behaviours that could potentially be causing all the unpleasantness that we see in our world, we are then applying a forceful antidote to them. The realization that it could be me who created the vile boss who screams at me incessantly, or the unfaithful partner, is the very remedy that ensures we will not repeat the causes for such unhappiness.

The most powerful antidote is the deep relief that comes with the understanding that "I can change my pain"! We get to stop waiting for our boss to finally give us some kudos, or for our partners to give us what we want! Cool. Very cool. Not to mention ultimately empowering.

The deep meditation that grows from
The fertile field of careful examination
Is food for the serious practitioner.
Master Shantideva, *Guide to the Bodhisattva's Way of Life*

As Sally Fallon says,

It is the loving heart who will find, in the pages that follow, guidelines for providing an abundance of all the nutrients we need to live healthy, happy and productive lives.

Applying Mindfulness

Once I started compiling recipes and putting this book together, I realized that I actually had another ulterior motive, aside from using the Six Perfections to write a cookbook. I wanted to pass on some of our experiences with food and the effects of its preparation. We experienced firsthand how some foods could be detrimental to our health and practice, while others were highly beneficial. *The Hatha Yoga Pradipika,* the 16th century treatise on yogic practice by Master Swatmarama, which was one of our main retreat bibles, stresses purity and digestibility of food as paramount, along with quantity and personal preferences. It pays particular attention to what and how much a yogi should eat while in deep practice. In fact, it lists overeating as number one on the list of serious obstacles to spiritual practice!

We have experienced firsthand the effects of eating too much and eating foods which seemed bad for us: white sugar; white flour and highly processed and refined foods; white rice; packaged foods of any description; vegetables, fruits and other foods which are treated with pesticides and other chemical toxins; eggs from chickens raised by the thousands in batteries of cages who are fed commercial grain preparations; dairy products from cows that are severely mistreated in order to drastically increase the production of their milk, such as killing their babies and keeping the milk intended for them for ourselves. Many of these foods carry a stigma, a harmful pranic residue. They contain known toxins or are acquired through highly toxic processing methods or inhumane means. Knowingly eating them may produce undesirable results in our systems if we have a predisposition or karmic propensity to sensitivity from food.

Peacock Bodhisattvas

Why do some of us appear to have a high degree of sensitivity to food, while others seem to be like Peacock Bodhisattvas? They're called that, because like peacocks, known to be able to eat poisonous plants with no ill effects, Peacock Bodhisattvas can eat and do things that would be harmful to most people. Food allergies and sensitivities could have developed from overexposure to non-organic food and/or environmental toxins over the course of our lives, causing a chemical buildup that reaches a high level, so we cannot tolerate much more. Some people, however, seem to have inborn allergies or immediate reactions to certain substances. Here in deep retreat, we quickly noticed several things.

The quantity of food we ate seemed to have a direct correlation to our meditation and other practices, particularly pranayama and mudra/bandha practices. Even one mouthful too much made it impossible to meditate or practice, and we soon learned to gauge our appestat correctly. When are we full?

Yogic science says that our stomachs, which are approximately the size of the foot section of one of our own socks, should be half filled with food, a quarter with water, and the other quarter should be left empty. We found this to be a learning experience. In our culture, we eat for sport, pleasure, comfort, companionship, etc., but not necessarily for the optimal sustenance of a healthy body, mind, and life!

The quality and purity of our food also seemed to take on a heightened significance. Throughout our deep retreat we had the very great pleasure and good fortune to avail ourselves of the services of SPUD, our organic produce and grocery delivery company. They left our weekly bin chock full of delicious organic food, and kindly took any outgoing mail!

While all the produce they delivered was organic, much of it came from California and Mexico. We noticed a big difference in the quality of produce we had grown in our own vegetable garden, which we picked, washed, and ate within minutes, and the produce that had to travel a long way to get to us. There is a live taste, a greenness that only comes with the freshest food.

We have always noticed a huge difference in the taste of organically grown produce vs. any other—its intensity of flavour severely diminishes with the application of chemicals and toxic fertilizers. We've now become very sensitized to the chemical aftertaste of many non-organic fruits and vegetables.

We also noticed an extraordinary difference in eggs, which both of us find very nourishing and satisfying as one of our main sources of protein and high quality vitamins and minerals. One of our neighbours a few doors down raised chickens and sold the eggs at a roadside stand on an honour system (leave your money in the jar and take your eggs). These eggs had

the deepest orange colour of yolks (like carrots!) and the thickest, most viscous whites we had ever seen! And their taste, amazing. Those chickens are eating whatever chickens eat when they get to roam around freely. They are looked after as pets! We could really taste a difference in their eggs, which we got to eat within a day or two, sometimes within hours, of those hens laying them. The only problem was that those Hess Road hens didn't always lay eggs just because we happened to run out. It was a source of great adventure and excitement for us to walk down the road to see whether there were any eggs (there's not *that* much to do in long term, isolated, deep retreat!).

Another major food in our staple diet was organic dairy products in small amounts—non-homogenized yogurt, organic butter, raw milk cheeses. We wished we could purchase a cow share and have access to raw milk, which is infinitely superior in nutritional content and taste, but the law in British Columbia requires pasteurization of milk for commercial sale, which inevitably destroys many beneficial enzymes.

What we did notice, though, was a dramatic difference in the taste and colour of even organic butters from different parts of the world. Avalon Organic Butter comes from B.C. dairy farms, and is a deep yellow colour—absolutely delicious. Other organic butters are much paler by comparison. We have learned from studying Dr. Weston Price's amazing and informative book *Nutrition and Physical Degeneration* that cows who are free to roam and feed exclusively on extremely rich pasture—like B.C. pastures in the spring after a winter of constant rain—produce an extraordinary component in their milk which he discovered and calls *Activator X*. This produces the deep, rich, yellow colour, and is a powerful catalyst for inducing the body to absorb and utilize minerals like vitamins A and D. But when the cows are fed any soy-based feeds, hay, or cottonseed meal, *Activator X* disappears!

THE BODHISATTVA'S PANTRY

What we ate quickly became a big issue. We noticed that any increased consumption of white, unrefined sugar produced an imbalance in the body and mind—a sort of wired feeling which was quickly followed by a state of depression, the severity of which depended on how much white sugar we had eaten! We learned to replace it completely with naturally occurring sweeteners like date or prune pulp, or juice, raisins, bananas, coconut sugar, rapadura, stevia powder, molasses, raw honey, or maple syrup in addition to sharply decreasing our consumption of sweeteners overall. We often decreased the sweetener called for in recipes by 50% or more.

Excessive consumption of highly refined wheat and grain products (like most crackers, white bread, white rice, white flour pasta, etc.) seemed to produce the same effect as refined sugar, as well as a feeling of bloating in the belly and swelling in the joints—knees, hips, shoulders, ankles. We also noticed that excessive intake of carbohydrates and starchy foods (white rice, potatoes) and insufficient protein intake produced similar effects.

We think that the less a product has been handled, processed, and touched by mankind, the better. We'll share with you the short list of foods we ate and continue to eat daily, foods we ate occasionally, foods we rarely ate, and foods we try not to eat at all.

To give you an idea of what we consider essential foods, we thought we'd just reproduce our weekly grocery list. This is what SPUD delivered to us on Wednesdays, along with a few weekly special surprises that we never knew about since we had no Internet.

apples	each	6
arugula or other salad greens	bunch	1
avocados	each	3
bananas	each	6
basil or other herbs	bunch	1
beets	1 lb	1
berries, assorted, when available	pkg	1
broccoli	bunch	1
cabbage: bok choy, napa, red or white	each	1
cantaloupe, mango, melon or other	each	1
carrots	bunch	1
cauliflower	each	1
celery	bunch	1
chard	bunch	1
cilantro	bunch	1
collard greens	bunch	1
cucumber, eggplant, zucchini, or other veg in season	each	1
Ezekiel organic sesame sprouted bread	loaf	1
ginger	1/4 lb	1
grapefruit or oranges	each	2
green onions	bunch	1
kale	bunch	2
kiwis or other fruit in season	each	1
lemons	each	3

PADMA YVONNE JAQUES

limes	each	3
mushrooms: button, shiitake or other	1/2 lb	1
organic brown rice pasta	pkg	1
organic butter	1 lb	1
organic corn or sprouted grain tortillas	pkg	1
organic cream	500 ml	1
organic half-and-half cream	500 ml	1
organic milk	1 L	1
organic tofu	pkg	1
organic yogurt, plain non-homogenized 3.5%	650 g	1
other seasonal veg	bunch	1
parsley	bunch	1
pears	each	4
peppers, turnips, or other veg in season	each	1
pineapple, bunch of grapes or other	each	1
potatoes, sweet	1 lb	1
potatoes, white	1 lb	1
pumpkin or other squash when available	each	1
spinach	bunch	1
strawberries when available	punnet	1
tomatoes	1/2 lb	1

Foods We Enjoyed Every Day

Eggs

Source the highest quality eggs available, organic or free range. Eggs are a great source of protein and much needed fat-soluble vitamins. The chickens should really be free range and omnivores; all vegetarian feed creates an imbalance in the omega-3 and 6 ratios, which then reflects in us. Until we have set the correct forces in motion to enable chickens to be happy, healthy vegetarians, we don't feel that it's right to mess with their natural dietary inclinations. We did, though, read about an Indian guru who trained his lion to be a vegetarian! (*Autobiography of a Yogi* by Paramahansa Yogananda)

Organic dairy products/raw milk products

We had trouble sourcing raw milk, otherwise we would have used it exclusively. Raw milk and raw milk products are a vital source of the fat-soluble vitamins and enzymes needed for proper cellular functions. In the meantime, the only true raw (raw meaning unpasteurized) product legally available on the market is cheese. Yogurt is heated and cooked, thus killing the fat-soluble vitamins. We used only organic whole milk and cream. We enjoyed a wonderful non-homogenized yogurt called Cream Top in small amounts just about daily. Saugeen Country Dairy also makes a delicious organic non-homogenized yogurt from whole milk.

Butter and oils

Organic is best because toxins, antibiotics, hormones, and all the things they feed into cows these days are carried or bound into fat molecules. High-vitamin butter is a deep rich yellow colour and comes in spring and fall with the fresh heavy pasture. Organic butters don't have additives or colourants either. Butter and other healthy fats are vital on a daily basis for good cellular structure and function but only butter, cream, or other animal fats, such as in egg yolks, allows us to absorb many fat-soluble vitamins that can't otherwise be assimilated. We also ate nut butters and used ghee, toasted sesame seed oil, and organic cold-pressed olive oils for cooking. We loved raw unrefined coconut oil—amazing, delicious, and super healthful. The brand of coconut oil we used is called Nutiva Organic Extra Virgin Coconut Oil. Both coconut oil and butter have been found to promote good brain development, strong bones, and have anti-microbial and anti-carcinogenic properties as well. Both are also less likely to cause weight gain than polyunsaturated oils. This was especially interesting to us. How is it that in a country with an obesity epidemic like the United States we were often unable to find full-fat yogurt because the shelves are lined with 0% fat yogurt and 0% fat cream?

PADMA YVONNE JAQUES

Breads, grains and/or cereals

We only ate sprouted grain or homemade sourdough breads—vastly superior to white flour breads. Whole-wheat breads contain a mass of vitamins and minerals which are contained in the outer sheath of the wheat (white flour removes this sheath). We enjoyed Ezekiel brand sesame sprouted grain bread and sprouted grain tortillas. The sprouting process enhances the nutritional qualities and removes the phytates which block nutrient absorption. We ate only organic brown rice—Lundberg brand is delicious. We soaked the rice for 7 hours first, then drained and fried the rice grains in butter or coconut oil before adding water and cooking. Other grains we alternated between were quinoa, sprouted whole-wheat berries, sprouted buckwheat, amaranth, kamut, millet, and oats. We either pre-soaked and sprouted, or at the very least, pre-soaked. We soaked most grains, legumes, and nuts in water for anywhere from 7 to 24 hours before cooking or eating, as this neutralized phytates which are present in most grains.

Salt

We used only grey, unrefined, unbleached French sea salt or pink fine ground rock salt from the Himalayas.

Fruit/vegetables

We only ate organic or from our garden. If you don't, here is a list, according to the Earth Watch Group, of the fruit and vegetables that you should buy organic, due to high levels of pesticide residues.

Apples	Lettuce
Bell peppers	Nectarines
Blueberries	Peaches
Celery	Potatoes
Grapes	Spinach
Kale/collards	Strawberries

Each day we ate a large portion of greens and one full-fruit meal a day. As you can see from our grocery list, this was in addition to generous portions of a wide variety of vegetables. We had a really good power salad at least twice a week for a big boost in enzymes and nutrients. We included raw avocado and beets often, and only used cold-pressed olive oil, freshly-squeezed lemon or lime juice, and balsamic vinegar for dressing. We never used commercially produced dressings.

Pure water and a little tea with whole milk

We were so fortunate to be where we were as we had a well and our water tested exceedingly pure. If yours doesn't, it is wise to install a water filter.

High quality dark chocolate

We had one piece a day, usually after lunch.

Foods We Often Ate

Nuts and seeds

Nuts and seeds are best pre-soaked for 24 hours, then toasted to a crispy state in a very low temperature oven overnight. They are great for snacks, nut milks, nut creams, salads, nut butters, baking, and pestos. Soaking neutralizes phytates and enzyme blockers that prohibit nutrient absorption. It also works to increase digestibility and prevent bloating. Homemade nut milks and creams are a delicious and wonderful alternative to dairy milk and cream. We often used them in recipes instead of dairy milk. Most nuts contain natural oils that prevent the onset of rancidity, especially if they have been pre-soaked and toasted, but walnuts are an exception, and should be refrigerated.

Fermented soy products and tofu

Miso soup was popular in our house. We also used miso in other dishes, sauces, and dressings. We ate tofu in very small amounts as it is only partially fermented and we found we weren't able to easily digest large amounts.

Spices and herbs

Organic, non-irradiated spices and herbs are best. We also used herbs from our large herb garden.

Legumes, pulses, and beans

We ate different varieties of lentils several times a week and beans like azuki, pinto, garbanzo, or black beans less frequently. We always pre-soaked and often sprouted these prior to cooking, as well as skimming off the foam once we started cooking. Once soaked, slice a bean in half. If the centre is still opaque, soak for longer. Adding a two-inch piece of kombu (dried seaweed) to the cooking water seems to make beans easier to digest. Other digestive spices are bay leaves, cumin, and fennel. When cooking beans: add salt, miso, soy sauce, tomatoes, or lemons after cooking, when beans are already soft. Otherwise they toughen uncooked beans and lengthen cooking time considerably. These methods ensure easier assimilation, digestibility, and that the enzyme inhibitors are neutralized. Beans and pulses are rich in minerals, B-complex, D vitamins, and contain several anti-cancer agents. All legumes contain both omega-3 and omega-6 fatty acids.

Cheese

We often cooked with cheese and although we would have loved to be eating raw milk cheeses exclusively, they are prohibitively expensive. Cheeses produced from whole organic milk are second best, especially if the milk is from cows that are fed only grass. Many cheeses imported from Europe, such as Parmesan, are made from the raw milk of grass fed cows.

Foods We Occasionally Ate

Natural sweeteners

We occasionally enjoyed maple syrup, raw honey, coconut sugar, or naturally occurring high sugar foods such as dates, raisins, prunes, and dried apricots.

Herb teas, pure cocoa, and coffee

We indulged in these only on very special occasions during our deep retreat. Mostly we just drank pure water.

Foods We Rarely Ate

Garlic and onions

These foods are too intense and difficult to digest for a pair of aspiring yogis trying to meditate! They are highly stimulating and seemed to give us bloating and gas.

White flour and white rice

We only ate these in very small amounts and we always used organic unbleached white flour. Anita's and Grandma Nunweiler are two great brands we've tried. White flour foods that we avoided included bread, pasta, crackers, and so on. White rice and white flour have been stripped of most of their nutrients which are found in the husk.

Foods We Tried To Avoid

Canned fruits or vegetables

We had no need to eat these, and nutritional value can't compare to fresh.

MSG

This is a big neurotoxin. Obesity, eye damage, headaches, fatigue, disorientation, depression, numbness, burning sensation, tingling, facial pressure or tightness, chest pain or difficulty breathing, headache, nausea, rapid heartbeat, drowsiness, and weakness have been linked to MSG.

Baking powder

Baking powder contains aluminum oxide, which stops it from clumping and is directly linked to Alzheimer's disease. Instead, we used baking soda or eggs as leavening. Pre-soaking flours in yogurt, whey, or lemon water for 24 hours makes them rise better. If you are baking with alternative grains, you can make your own baking powder to use in addition to baking soda: 2 parts potassium bicarbonate (available from your pharmacist), 2 parts cream of tartar and 2 parts arrowroot powder. Store in an airtight glass jar. Use 2 tsp (10 ml) of homemade baking powder per cup of alternative grain flour, such as buckwheat, rye, barley, oat, corn, rice, millet, amaranth, quinoa, or lentil flours.

Refined white sugar or artificial sweeteners

Refined white sugar comes in many forms, such as dextrose, corn syrup, and fructose. Brown sugar is refined sugar from which all nutrients have been removed with a little molasses added back in to give it its colour. Refined sugars set up acidic conditions in the body which can contribute to premature aging and are now linked to a host of inflammatory conditions and degenerative diseases including cancer. Since we mostly

eliminated these from our diet, we found we didn't crave or need sugar as long as we were eating a properly balanced diet rich in fat-soluble vitamins and proteins. We also didn't drink concentrated fruit juices or soft drinks, which contain artificial sweeteners. Aspartame is the most widely used and contains neurotoxins which can cause dizziness, impaired vision, severe muscular pain, numbing of extremities, high blood pressure, retinal hemorrhage, seizures, depression, chemical disruptions in the brain, and birth defects! Before we started retreat, we remember not being able to find ANY chewing gum that didn't contain aspartame. We also checked toothpaste and dental floss labels carefully—many contain aspartame, as well.

Iodized free flowing white table salt

This type of salt has been stripped of its minerals, bleached, and chemically treated. Fine ground aluminum oxides are then added to make it flow. Aluminum is directly linked to Alzheimer's disease and nervous system disorders.

Synthetic vitamins

We have never taken vitamin supplements. It is very difficult for the body to assimilate these and make any kind of functional use of them, and they end up stressing our excretory organs.

Fast food/snacks

We avoided these and feel that they negate any good aspects of the high quality food we were eating! Even organic corn chips are fried in highly refined vegetable oils, which are responsible for many medical ailments including heart disease. The high temperature cooking chemically alters the oil, creating a host of free radicals and turns it into a neurotoxin.

Commercial, dry, boxed cereals

We particularly avoided anything produced by the extrusion process, which is how they make the small flakes and shapes. These are formed at high temperatures and pressure, which destroy many valuable nutrients in grains, causing oils to become rancid and renders some of the proteins toxic.

Hydrolyzed protein or any soy-based food products

Traditionally, fermented soy products (miso, tempeh, and natto) and partially fermented soy foods like tofu should be eaten only in very small quantities as a side dish or accompaniment, as they are in Japan. In this form, they promote digestion and a healthy intestinal tract. But when the soy protein is not fermented and is instead isolated and concentrated, as in soy milk and some vegetable burgers, the high levels of phytic acid which block the absorption of minerals and other vital nutrients, isoflavones, and enzyme inhibitors can produce serious gastric distress, reduced protein digestion, and chronic deficiencies in the absorption of amino acids. There also seems to be a link to thyroid problems.

Highly processed vegetable oils of any kind

Margarines, tub spreads, fat substitutes, food fried in vegetable oils (potato chips, corn chips—even organic ones!), or any reduced fat or non-fat products did not make it to our table. We avoided all hydrogenated fats and oils like safflower, corn, sunflower, soybean, and cottonseed oils, as these start out with an imbalance of omega-3 and omega-6 fatty acids as well as being very highly refined. They often end up being toxic for human consumption. Free radicals form with certain groups of proteins during processing and are destructive to cellular membranes. Many of these oils are also linked to heart disease.

Irradiated or genetically modified foods of any kind

Studies show that irradiated food, besides glowing in the dark(!) causes mutagenic blood abnormalities. Most commercially sold spices are irradiated to prevent sprouting, so check labels carefully. Kirlian imaging, a method of photographing the energetic or pranic patterns of a substance or a person, shows that fresh fruits and vegetables shine with light radiating out an inch or more in an aura with vibrant patterns. Irradiated food, on the other hand, has virtually no light halo and has significantly altered energetic patterns.

Skim milk or milk powder

Organic or not, these are highly processed foods which have gone through extremely high temperatures. This effectively destroys all the microbial organisms, leaving the milk inert and toxic to the human digestive tract. This can cause lactose intolerance, allergies, and a whole host of other issues. The skimming process strips the milk of essential saturated fats, fat-soluble vitamins A, D, and K2, and healthy cholesterol.

Having said all that, we do have friends who can eat many of the foods that we find produce negative effects in our systems—that's those Peacock Bodhisattvas again! We aspire to being like that— able to eat anything, whatever is around—and be nourished by it, without having to concern ourselves with our delicate little bodies! Until we create the causes to be sustained by anything at all, we fuss around and try to learn and pass on what seems to help us and, we hope, you.

How do we create the causes to become Peacock Bodhisattvas? We ponder what a relief it must be not to have to worry about ourselves, to simply be available for others. Contemplating how liberating this would be and emulating the way Peacock Bodhisattvas do things takes us a long way towards this goal.

> May I be like those named Gentle Voice
> [Manjushri, Buddha of Wisdom]
> And all the others...

I make supplication with my
palms joined at my heart,
To the totally enlightened
beings, and Bodhisattvas,
Who reside in every direction of the world,
To those beings who possess great compassion.
The Victorious Buddhas, the
Saviours of all living kind,
Exert themselves in order to protect beings.
Thus it is that you should take refuge today itself,
In those of great power, who
remove every kind of fear.
I rejoice in the enlightenment
of those who protect...
I rejoice with gladness in the ocean
Of the goodness of the wish for enlightenment
Which brings every living being to happiness;
I rejoice too in what they undertake
To help all living kind.
I pray that I may become myself
A great treasure house,
One that can never be exhausted,
For all living beings who are poor, and lack.
May I become too anything they need
Or want, an entire range
Of the different necessities for life,
And so appear to their very eyes.

Master Shantideva, *Guide to the Bodhisattva's Way of Life*

MINDFUL PREPARATION

HOW WE PREPARED OUR FOOD SEEMED TO dramatically change its taste and effects on us. For example, we learned from Sally Fallon's wonderful book *Nourishing Traditions* how to pre-soak unrefined grains like whole-wheat flour to release enzyme-blocking phytates which are contained in most grains and flours, making them much more easily digestible. Digestibility can become a big issue in deep retreat as physical body systems slow right down while in prolonged states of deep meditation. Pre-soaking in water or in yogurt or buttermilk for 12 to 24 hours to induce fermentation also totally changes the consistency of 100% whole-wheat breads and cakes, eliminating the heaviness which we typically associate with 100% whole-wheat anything. Soaking whole-wheat flour, corn flour, buckwheat flour, and other whole grains for 24 hours also makes them rise better.

We also pre-soaked nuts, then toasted them in an oven at 150 to 175°F (65 to 80°C) for 6 to 8 hours or until crisp and fragrant. We found this prevented the heaviness and bloated feeling you can get from eating nuts, which can be quite difficult to digest. In fact, I now pre-soak all my grains (buckwheat, wheat berries, whole-wheat flour, rice, amaranth, millet, quinoa, barley, and others) and legumes (lentils, beans) as well.

Allowing many of these grains and legumes to sprout provides many added benefits as well, including producing vitamin C, increasing B vitamin content, and carotene content. More importantly, sprouting our legumes and grains also neutralized phytic acid (which blocks the absorption of calcium and magnesium) just as soaking does, enabling our own digestive enzymes to survive and do their job. In addition to decomposing certain sugars which cause intestinal gas, sprouting increases enzyme activity by as much as six times!

Master Swatmarama mentions in the *The Hatha Yoga Pradipika* that leftover food that has been sitting around for a while, even in the refrigerator, loses its prana or life-giving force. We couldn't always consume everything we cooked in one sitting, but we tried to use up our leftovers as quickly as we could. Otherwise, we immediately froze them. Our teacher once said a good guideline is to leave it out at room temperature and eat it before it goes bad!

THE MINDFUL COOK

WE ALL NEED TO MAKE OUR OWN DECISIONS about what foods or ingredients we will or will not use, both from an ethical standpoint and otherwise. This book contains ovo-lacto vegetarian recipes. We ate dairy products and eggs, but were extremely careful about sourcing these. Becoming a happy vegetarian or vegan requires realizations specific to each individual. It cannot be forced and our experience is that a slow integration of new foods is a sensible way to go. Weaning ourselves gently off foods we have eaten for a lifetime and then very slowly and gradually introducing others mitigates shock to our systems.

Dr. Price's research, documented in *Nutrition and Physical Degeneration,* took him to every corner of the globe in the 1930s to study the traditional diets and health of primitive races of people before and after modern processed food reached them. His research showed that the more that processed and refined foods were introduced into the diets of these people, the more their health suffered. When they exclusively ate their traditional diets, whatever that might be—carnivorous, omnivorous, or herbivorous—they enjoyed health, vitality, great vigour, and a physical attractiveness that was astonishing. He also mentions a remarkable correlation between radically increasing the intake of pure, unadulterated food with proper proportions of nutrients, and an accompanying decrease in sociopathic and criminal behaviours, even an increase in highly ethical behaviours.

Today's fast-paced world takes just as much of a toll on the reserves of the human organism as the intense work that yogis and yoginis practice in long, isolated retreat with their body/mind complex. Basically, we could say that when the human organism is operating at peak efficiency, it allows our subtle or inner body energies to flow freely. Because this subtle energy (known as wind, prana, chi, ki) rides in tandem with our minds, inseparably, the thoughts too can be elevated to a higher, more altruistic level. This state can happen spontaneously as a result of cleaning out the body and providing it with the highest quality raw materials it needs to reach that state.

You don't have to be in long, isolated retreat to practice. Our whole life is a practice, a struggle to find balance not only within ourselves but also to then extend that harmony into our families and into the world in general. Being healthy shouldn't be an accident, but unfortunately for the vast majority of us it is. In our current condition there is no control over our health, no surefire way to guarantee it. So, in that sense, when one has good health it could be construed as luck.

In fact, that is exactly how Eastern medical traditions like the Tibetan doctors define health—a somewhat lucky and accidental state that cannot last. Having premium health and vitality allows us to contribute and assist others in the world, whether it is our close family and friends, or a wider circle of needy members of our communities, locally or on a global scale. And, while good health doesn't guarantee happiness, it does provide a stable platform of well-being that can be developed and then taught to others. Fine tuning our diet automatically triggers a deeper awareness of the sufferings of all beings.

How does that work?

If food is the cause for this elevated awareness, then it would have to follow that everyone who ate the same group of high quality foods of the right kind would reach that place. This is sadly not the case. If only we could eat our way to enlightenment! Judging by the chronic incidence of obesity in the world today, one could be forgiven for thinking many people are trying desperately to do just that. Maybe so, but the approach just needs a little fine tuning. The ultimate destiny and deep yearning of every being is to reach that place where we can truly help others and make them happy.

Given the fact that both myself
And others are exactly the same
In wanting happiness,
What difference could there ever be
Between us, what reason that I work
Only for happiness for myself?
Given the fact that both myself
And others are exactly the same
In not wanting pain,
What difference could there ever be
Between us, what reason that I protect
Myself and not all others?

Master Shantideva, *Guide to the Bodhisattva's Way of Life*

Let's have a look at how the Bodhisattvas do it with the Six Perfections.

PADMA YVONNE JAQUES

THE SIX PERFECTIONS

The Perfection of Giving
The Perfection of Kindness
The Perfection of Patience
The Perfection of Joy in Making Great Effort
The Perfection of Concentration
The Perfection of Wisdom

MASTER SHANTIDEVA, WHOSE NAME means Peace Angel, was an 8th-century Indian prince turned monastic who wrote the Bodhisattvacharyavatara, Sanskrit *for Guide to the Bodhisattva's Way of Life*, which we quote extensively. This awe-inspiring piece of scripture has become the tour de force of how to understand and live the Six Perfections. It is one of His Holiness the 14th Dalai Lama's favourite texts for drawing inspiration for his many public teachings. It's the ultimate cookbook with the recipes that actually produce great results every time!

Geshe Michael often talks about the upward spiral of the Six Perfections. Practicing giving gradually cleans the body and mind of its obsession with getting things for itself. This paves the way to becoming acutely conscious of others and what they might need; which is the backbone of living ethically and kindly—never harming others or ourselves to get what we want or to avoid what we don't want.

Having this keen sense of restraining ourselves from negative actions naturally leads to the next perfection of not getting angry especially when the situation calls for it.

This stream of consciousness invites the sheer joy of simply making great effort doing wonderful things for others, which then feeds upon itself! The more kindness we show to others and the more we spend our lives for the benefit of many, the more joy we experience, and the more we are inspired to do for others.

These first four perfections make the mind and conscience completely clear. Without this clarity and transparency, there is no hope of concentration. Have you ever tried to meditate after having denied someone something they desperately needed? Or after having been deliberately nasty to your partner? After having a horrendous screaming match with a close friend? Or after spending the day resentfully doing something for someone and watching the clock the whole time? We found it hard enough to meditate on Wednesday afternoons when we were anticipating SPUD delivering our weekly grocery bin!

Cleaning up our act is vital to perfecting concentration and then using that concentration to meditate on: the true nature of how things work; the true causes

of things; the consistent, reliable, dependable, and reproducible causes for happiness; the elimination of suffering; perpetual joy, and unconditional, protective equanimity for all beings. We have to perfect meditation in order to perfect wisdom in order to truly perfect giving, kindness, patience, and joy. Until that time, we practice. Practice what? The first five perfections, of course!

Understand first the fact that vision
Perfection of Wisdom
Married close to quietude
Perfection of Concentration and Meditation
Destroys the mental afflictions.
Begin by seeking quietude
Perfection of Concentration and Meditation;
It in turn is achieved by the bliss
Of losing attachment for the world
Perfections of Giving, Kindness,
Patience, and Joyful Effort

Master Shantideva, *Guide to the Bodhisattva's Way of Life*

Check it out. Don't take anything I say for granted. Like the recipes in this book, you'll never know if these ideas are any good unless you try them. They need to be tried and tested, preferably under clinical-trial type conditions!

If you get really serious about subjecting these ideas to rigorous testing in the laboratory of your own life, it would be best to journal your experiments and your findings. It will be easier to track your results.

We have a special method for doing this by tracing certain causes to certain results and entering our findings several times a day. For more information, our friends at Three Jewels Vancouver can show you. (www.threejewelsvancouver.com)

Like some of the recipes which require several days or longer to make, be ready for a time lapse between planting the seeds for food to nourish you (by consciously nourishing others) and experiencing the results of health and vitality. There is a time lag in this process, which is why we often see bad things happening to good people and vice versa. That's why it looks like the bank robber appeared to successfully make off with his heist and live happily ever after on a tropical island. The happily-ever-after part comes from a completely different cause, and the bank-robbery part has yet to produce its result. But one thing is for sure. Well, four things actually:

1. Good results can only come from good actions with good intentions. Bad results can only come from bad actions, made more powerful if the intention is conscious. (Oak trees can only grow from acorns, never from pumpkin seeds.)

2. All seeds grow.

3. If you plant the seed, you will get a result.

4. If you don't plant the seed, you cannot get a result.

Test it out by using this cookbook to practice this short list of some of the real root causes for health and vitality, the good seeds, to see whether they grow and manifest as health and vitality for you. If you try it and thereby plant the seed, you'll definitely get the result. If you don't try it and therefore don't plant the seed, you absolutely can't get the result.

1. Grow organic produce for those who don't have a garden or can't afford it. *The Perfection of Giving*

2. Cook nutritious, high-quality food for others. *The Perfection of Giving*

3. Go out of your way not to hurt other beings, for example, don't bake with white sugar or use highly processed vegetable oils when preparing food for others. They might be diabetic or be susceptible to heart disease. *The Perfection of Kindness*

4. At every opportunity, protect life. For instance, check your produce thoroughly for living things, and remove any you find carefully before washing and cooking. *The Perfection of Kindness*

5. Notice that food prepared when our minds are highly afflicted is tainted and doesn't taste as good. *The Perfection of Patience*

6. Consciously infuse your food with love and consciously move beyond any impatience or annoyance while preparing food. *The Perfection of Patience*

7. Make efforts to joyfully attend to people who are sick or needy; people who have addictions; people who are dying, perhaps by offering them special meals to suit them and please them. *The Perfection of Joy in Making Great Effort*

8. Help others achieve excellent health by sharing your time and your knowledge and these ideas with them. *The Perfection of Joy in Making Great Effort*

9. Use your food preparation time as an opportunity for silent contemplation and meditation. Use some of the meditations in this book as you prepare food. *The Perfection of Concentration and Meditation*

10. Use the meditations in this book as a short form of grace, shifting your body and mind into a relaxed and happy state before eating. *The Perfection of Concentration and Meditation*

11. Recall constantly as you cook and eat that in order for our food to nourish us, we must have been actively involved in nourishing others—the only true cause of good health from our food. *The Perfection of Concentration and Meditation*

12. When we consciously perform these root causes a seed or imprint is planted in our minds, and when it grows, it becomes the very Perfection that we have given to others. This also has the remarkable effect of clearing away any causes we have already created which would otherwise have produced a negative result for us. *All of the Perfections*

CHAPTER 1

The Perfection of Giving: Vegetables and Salads

It was spoken that the perfection
Of giving is the thought to give all that one has,
Along with the results,
To every living being.
This then is the reason why
It's the state of mind alone.

Since they have stopped bad deeds,
They feel no pain; and because
They are wise, there's no dislike.
This is due to the fact that thinking of things
The wrong way, and doing negative deeds,
Harm the body and mind.

Master Shantideva, *Guide to the Bodhisattva's Way of Life*

Contemplation:

1. Imagine all the people who worked so hard to get our food to you, from the farmer to the delivery person or cashier at the supermarket.
2. Visualize gratitude as it streams out from your heart to theirs in the form of brilliant rays of sunlight, which illuminate the entire planet, basking it in the love and light it needs for crops to grow and feed us all.
3. Offer the food you are about to eat or prepare to those who live in constant fear of not having enough food, resources, shelter, or love.

THE PERFECTION OF GIVING INVOLVES THE giving of any material thing to others who might need it and the giving of teachings or any information that improves the life of another and increases their happiness and contentment quotient. By providing protection from fear to all beings, such as by cultivating equanimity, we can automatically ensure that no being would need to fear us. We must also give love—unconditionally and without expectation.

The most powerful way of giving is to give things which you are reluctant to part with.

Ultimately, perfecting giving is the willingness to give anything that another being might need in order to get them to an enlightened state. Giving the way Peacock Bodhisattvas do might include, for example, giving praise to someone we are jealous of or giving significant material gifts anonymously.

Peacock Bodhisattvas are eventually able to give whatever it takes to bring another being higher. And what it takes is simply the Wish—altruistic unconditional limitless love for all beings. Scriptures provide extraordinary examples of Bodhisattvas clawing out their own eyeball and giving it to someone who was missing one, or breaking their own kneecaps and giving them to a handicapped person so they could walk. These exalted beings have risen beyond the karma of experiencing fear or pain from performing these outrageous acts of giving. That is to say, experiencing pain from taking out your eyeball is a karmic result of having inflicted pain on others in the past. It is possible to annihilate such karmas. That is the career path of the Bodhisattva. Until then, says Master Shantideva, take great joy in giving carrots and potatoes!

Vegetables and fruits that have been grown organically and therefore retain a higher degree of their nutritive qualities remind us of these Bodhisattvas. What they give to us—vitality, vitamins and minerals, fragrance and flavour, protection from harmful diseases—is their very essence! They grow, they yield their fruit or blossoms, and they die. If we don't partake of their offerings, they simply regenerate themselves into the earth and then come back again. This is truly the ultimate in generosity—an extraordinary example of the perfection of giving.

As we look around at the Peacock Bodhsiattvas we know, we notice that they want for nothing. Their lives are rich and full, perfectly contented. It has no bearing on their income level or their lifestyle. These are the results of attaining this perfection—they experience total abundance, a complete lack of scarcity in any area of their lives. Which then frees them up to be Peacock Bodhisattvas.

Another angle on perfecting giving is not consuming more than we need, whether it's food at the dinner table, paper from the toilet roll, water in the shower, oil from our earth, not firing up the big oven when we could use the toaster oven, and so on. This will always result in abundance.

Serving and giving away vegetables and herbs from our abundant gardens gives us great delight. It's such a gift of life. Try to consume and serve only organically grown produce. Heavily sprayed, commercially grown produce cannot compare in quality, taste or nutritional value to organic produce. Sally Fallon tells of a batch of oranges that tested zero in vitamin C due to having been grown in completely depleted soils—a result of intensive, commercial agricultural practices. See page XXI for a short list of vegetables that are best consumed organic as they test particularly high in residual pesticides.

DIAMOND FOREST RAINBOW SALAD

My mother always said to eat as many different coloured vegetables in a day as you can. Not only does this ensure a complete cross-section of all your vitamins, minerals, and other nutrients, but it is also truly a beautiful sight!

4 cups (1 L) salad greens (arugula, spring greens, mesclun or other)
2–4 tbsp (30–60 ml) olive oil, or to taste
1–2 (15–30 ml) tbsp balsamic vinegar, or to taste
sea salt and pepper, to taste
¼ cup (60 ml) blueberries
¼ cup (60 ml) julienned green, yellow, and red bell peppers

¼ cup (60 ml) grated beets
¼ cup (60 ml) grated carrots
¼ cup (60 ml) grated daikon
2 tbsp (30 ml) lemon juice, freshly squeezed
1/3 cup (80 ml) toasted almonds, slivered or sliced (optional)

3

Toss the greens in a large bowl with olive oil, balsamic vinegar, salt, and pepper. Top with the berries and vegetables. Pour lemon juice over the salad. Finally, top with the almonds.

CHARRED PEPPERS AND MUSHROOM SALAD

Serves 2–4

Bell peppers are capsicums—members of the nightshade family—making them cousins to eggplants, tomatoes, and potatoes. They are generous to us in their gifts of vitamin C, carotenoids, potassium, and calcium. Red peppers are richer in these than green ones.

Mushrooms give us protein, phosphorus, potassium, calcium, iron, B vitamins, and selenium. They are necessary for a healthy heart and circulatory system. They are composed of 90% water, which allows them to generously soak up the flavours of foods with which they are being cooked.

2 tbsp (30 ml) butter
½ each of green, orange, red, and yellow bell peppers, cut into thin strips
½ lb (250 g) of brown or shiitake mushrooms, sliced thickly

3 cups (750 ml) salad greens (arugula, spring greens, mesclun or other)
2 tbsp (30 ml) olive oil
1 tbsp (15 ml) lemon or lime juice
sea salt and pepper, to taste

Brown butter in a fry pan and sauté peppers until they are slightly charred. Remove from fry pan and add mushrooms, adding more butter as necessary. Allow the mushrooms to brown on one side before turning. Add the peppers back into the fry pan with the mushrooms briefly to reheat.

Toss the greens with the rest of the ingredients and serve in salad bowls. Place the peppers and mushrooms on top in each bowl. Serve while peppers and mushrooms are still hot.

4

MASSAGED KALE TOSS WITH BEETS AND ORANGES

SERVES 2–4

Kale is related to the cabbage family, which includes collards and mustard greens. All these verdant givers of life abundantly provide calcium, iron, carotenoids, and protect against cancer. They should always be cooked lightly to neutralize their oxalic acids.

1 bunch kale
2 tbsp (30 ml) olive oil or coconut
oil, warmed until liquid
1 tbsp (15 ml) lemon or lime
juice, freshly squeezed
sea salt, to taste
1 batch Lemony Beets (page 11)
1 orange, sliced thinly into
crescent shapes

Remove kale leaves from the tough stems. Chop roughly, then place in a bowl with the olive oil, lemon juice, and salt. Proceed to massage the kale pieces with your fingers for several minutes until they start to wilt and reduce—5 minutes or more. Sauté very briefly, no more than a minute.

Add the Lemony Beets and orange slices and toss.

SERVES 4–6

Our friend Madhuri created this gorgeous salad during an 11 day retreat we held for our students towards the very end of our deep retreat. She was inspired by a hand-balance asana class called The Float Point. The Float Point is essentially the place where we find a point of stillness and balance, the platform from which to fly. It changes the experience and possibly even the taste if you experiment with cutting vegetables in different shapes.

1 medium seedless cucumber
1 green zucchini
1 yellow zucchini
1 small daikon radish
3 tbsp (45 ml) rice vinegar

1 cup (250 ml) coconut milk
2 dates, pitted
1 cup (250 ml) almond butter
¼ cup (60 ml) toasted sesame oil

2 bunches kale, finely chopped
pinch of salt
2 tbsp (30 ml) coconut or sesame oil
2 carrots, grated

FOR THE SALAD:

2 tbsp (30 ml) sesame seeds
1 tbsp (15 ml) toasted sesame oil
1 tbsp (15 ml) maple syrup or
agave nectar (optional)
pinch of salt

FOR THE ALMOND-BUTTER SAUCE:

2–3 tbsp (30–45 ml) peeled and
grated fresh ginger
1½ tsp (7.5 ml) salt
juice of 1 lime

TO ASSEMBLE:

½ lb (250 g) rice noodles or soba noodles, boiled
until fully soft then soaked in cold water
¼ cup (60 ml) chopped fresh cilantro

For the salad base:

Use a spiral vegetable cutter or mandolin to create thin long strips of cucumber, zucchini, daikon radish, and combine in a bowl. Add rice vinegar, sesame seeds (reserving some for garnish), sesame oil, maple syrup, salt, and toss until coated. Refrigerate 2–6 hours to marinate.

For the almond-butter sauce:

Prepare almond butter sauce by blending coconut milk and dates in a blender until smooth. Stir in remaining sauce ingredients until well mixed. Strain well.

To assemble:

Sauté kale with a pinch of salt in oil until just cooked. Remove from heat and add in grated carrots. Toss in almond-butter sauce.

Place a layer of sauced kale at the bottom of each serving bowl. Top with a spiral nest of noodles and another spiral nest of the marinated vegetables. Garnish with the reserved sesame seeds and chopped cilantro.

LALI'S ROOT ROAST WITH GOAT CHEESE

SERVES 4–6

Brightly coloured root vegetables like yams and beets are intensely nutritious and sweet. They marry well with the bitter taste of brussels sprouts in this divine recipe from our friend Lali.

2 cups (500 ml) brussels sprouts, cut into halves and ends cut off

2 tbsp (30 ml) lemon juice

1 large or 2 small yams or sweet potatoes, peeled and cut into 1-inch (2.5 cm) cubes

2 beets, peeled and cut into 1-inch (2.5 cm) cubes

2 bell peppers, sliced into strips

2 tbsp (30 ml) coconut oil

½ tsp (2.5 ml) sea salt

¼ cup (60 ml) crumbled goat cheese

2–4 cups (500 ml–1 L) salad greens (arugula, spring greens, mesclun or other)

Preheat oven to 350°F (180°C). Mix the brussels sprouts with the lemon juice, then toss with the yams, beets, peppers, coconut oil, and salt. Bake for 40 minutes.

Toss the vegetables with the crumbled goat cheese while still hot out of the oven. Serve over a bed of greens.

BROCCOLI TIMBALES

This is a slight shift on Sally Fallon's delicious recipe in *Nourishing Traditions*. We add cheese to go with the broccoli, which is truly the king of nutrient providers in the vegetable world.

1 large bunch broccoli, stalks peeled and chopped roughly	¼ cup (60 ml) sour cream
1 cup (250 ml) grated cheese (pecorino, Parmesan, Asiago or your choice)	4 eggs, beaten
	1 green onion or ½ a leek, chopped finely
¼ cup (60 ml) butter, softened	sea salt and pepper, to taste

Preheat oven to 350°F (180°C). Steam-fry the broccoli with a little salt but only until tender-crisp. Don't allow it to change colour from its bright, verdant green.

Let the broccoli cool slightly and then put in a food processor or blender with the rest of the ingredients and blend until the broccoli and green onions are still visible as tiny chunks. Pour this batter into a well-buttered muffin pan or timbale moulds if you have them. Place the muffin pan into a pan of hot water, to poach the batter, and bake for about 15–20 minutes, or until a toothpick inserted comes out clean. Loosen the timbales with a knife and turn onto a plate.

These timbales are fine to make ahead of time and then reheat briefly in a toaster oven.

9

NUTTY GREEN BEANS

Serves 4–6

Green beans, cousins to dried legumes like peas and lentils, are high in calcium, potassium, and B-complex vitamins. They are higher in carotenoids and easier to digest than dried legumes. They are rich in alkaline-ash minerals.

2 tbsp (30 ml) coconut oil or butter
½ lb (250 g) string beans, green or yellow
sea salt, to taste
¼ cup (60 ml) almond butter

3 tbsp (45 ml) boiling water
1 tsp (5 ml) soy sauce
drizzle of maple syrup

Heat oil or butter in a fry pan. Add string beans and a dash of salt, lower heat, and cover until steam escapes.

Cook only a minute or so, until beans are tender but still a bright colour. Blend the remaining ingredients until smooth and pour over the beans.

LEMONY BEETS

Beets are an extraordinary vegetable with a glorious colour! They detoxify the blood and provide a therapeutic effect by restoring numerous bodily functions. Eating just a few spoonfuls of raw, cooked, or fermented beets each day ensures that you will get a good cross-section of vitamins and minerals—vitamin C, B-complex vitamins, carotene, calcium, iron, magnesium, phosphorus, copper, potassium, and sodium, to name a few! Fresh green beet tops are wonderful, and it's best that they accompany the beets into your belly as they have a synergistic relationship to one another. We like this very simple method of preparation, which preserves all the beet juices.

2–3 medium-sized beets
1 tbsp (15 ml) lemon juice, freshly squeezed
sea salt, to taste

Remove green tops and scrub beets until squeaky clean, but leave skins on. Wrap 2 or 3 at a time into a tinfoil pouch, rolling the 2 sets of corners tightly together to form a seal with all the seams at the top of the beets, and none at the bottom where the juices could spill out. Bake in a toaster oven at 400°F (200°C) for about an hour, or until you can insert a fork or toothpick easily. Now the skins just slip off! Slice into a bowl, pour lemon juice over, and toss gently with a little salt.

11

CABBAGE SAUTÉ

Serves 4–6

Cabbage furnishes us with vitamin C, B-complex vitamins, potassium, magnesium, calcium, fibre, and indoles; which protect against cancer. Because raw cabbage contains substances that inhibit the absorption of vitamin A, eat it cooked more frequently than raw.

1 tsp (5 ml) coriander seeds
3 tbsp (45 ml) coconut oil
½ head white cabbage, finely shredded

1 tbsp (15 ml) freshly grated ginger
1 tbsp (15 ml) dried coconut
sea salt, to taste

Fry the coriander seeds in heated coconut oil until they emit a lovely fragrance. Add the cabbage and cook until it starts to wilt and reduce in size, several minutes. Add the ginger and the dried coconut, stirring and cooking until the cabbage is tender and thoroughly cooked.

12

MAMA HILDE'S SWEET AND SOUR RED CABBAGE (WITH A TWIST)

SERVES 4–6

The life-giving benefits of red cabbage are the same as those of white cabbage, but its taste is a little stronger. I love serving this unusual European version of red cabbage inspired by my mother who friends refer to as Mama Hilde. Children of all ages seem to love it.

1 leek or 2 green onions, finely sliced
¼ cup (60 ml) butter
½ head red cabbage, finely sliced or shredded
2 apples, peeled, cored and finely sliced
3 tbsp (45 ml) organic apple cider vinegar

2–3 tbsp (30–45 ml) honey or maple syrup, to taste
1 tbsp (15 ml) freshly-squeezed lemon juice
1 bay leaf
sea salt, to taste

Sauté leek slices and butter in a big pot. Add the red cabbage and apples and cook until the cabbage starts to wilt. Add the rest of the ingredients and bring to a vigorous boil, stirring frequently. Lower heat and simmer for 45 minutes to an hour, until all liquid has completely evaporated.

SWEET POTATO AND JALAPEÑO SALAD

SERVES 6–8

The sublime sweet potato gives us more beta-carotene than any other vegetable! This compound bestows protection from cancer, colds, infections, and other diseases. That's not all. These jewels also give us iron, potassium, niacin, and vitamin C. Sweet potatoes are rich in fibre and very generous with their provision of vitamin B6, which is highly protective against heart disease. That's still not all! Sweet potatoes provide magnesium—another major player in heart-disease prevention. The carotene content of sweet potatoes increases with cold storage through the winter but our bodies can only convert carotene to vitamin A in the presence of animal fats such as the ones found in butter, egg yolks, or cream.

Jalapeños and other chilli peppers give us magnesium. They're also great for loosening phlegm, which is a Godsend for sufferers of chronic bronchitis or emphysema.

3–4 sweet potatoes or yams

2 tbsp (30 ml) chopped cilantro

2 tbsp (30 ml) finely sliced green onions

2 tbsp (30 ml) lime juice, freshly squeezed

1 tbsp (15 ml) olive or liquefied coconut oil

½ fresh or pickled jalapeño pepper, seeded and finely chopped

sea salt, to taste

Bake the sweet potatoes in a toaster oven at 375–400°F (190–200°C) for 45 minutes to an hour, depending on the size of the potatoes. Test for doneness by inserting a toothpick.

Peel the potatoes and chop them into bite-size pieces. Toss with the rest of the ingredients. Serve at room temperature or slightly warmed to melt the coconut oil (if using).

Lighter coloured squash and deeper coloured pumpkin varieties gift us with so much goodness: carotenoids, vitamin C, potassium, calcium, and fibre. Pair with nuts to up the protein content and contrast the flavours.

¼ cup (60 ml) pecans	sea salt, to taste
½ butternut squash, seeded	2 tbsp (30 ml) butter

Soak pecans overnight in salt water, drain and toast at 175°F (80°C) for 8–12 hours. Roughly chop the pecans and set aside.

Wrap squash, unpeeled, into a tinfoil pouch, rolling the 2 sets of corners tightly together to form a seal with all the seams at the top of the squash, and none at the bottom where the juices could spill out. Bake in a toaster oven at 375°F (190°C) for about an hour or until you can insert a fork or toothpick easily.

Peel the cooked squash and cube it into a bowl. Mix gently with the pecans, salt, and butter.

MUZZY'S CHEESY CAULIFLOWER

SERVES 6–8

Cauliflower gives us fibre and minerals as well as biotin, one of the B vitamins essential for our bodies to produce healthy fat. There are studies that show that cauliflower may protect against colon cancer as well. This recipe comes from Roger's mother whom we affectionately called Muzzy.

1 head cauliflower, chopped into small florets
1 leek or green onion, sliced thinly
3 tbsp (45 ml) butter
1½ tbsp (22.5 ml) unbleached flour
1 cup (250 ml) whole milk, heated

1 cup (250 mL) grated cheese (any kind you like)
sea salt, to taste
1 tbsp (15 ml) dried bread crumbs (optional)
2 tbsp (30 ml) fresh mixed herbs,
finely chopped (your choice)

Preheat oven to 350°F (180°C).

Steam-fry cauliflower and leek in butter until slightly browned. Remove the cauliflower and set aside.

Add flour to the buttery leeks and stir until it has been absorbed into the butter, adding more butter if necessary, to make a smooth roux. Add the heated milk and stir again until the sauce is smooth and free of lumps. To reduce the amount of dairy in this recipe, you could substitute vegetable stock for the milk.

Add the cheese and salt, and add the cauliflower back in, stirring constantly until the sauce is completely smooth and silky.

Transfer to a baking dish and sprinkle with bread crumbs. Top with the herbs and bake for about 15–20 minutes until bread crumbs are browned or mixture is just starting to bubble.

CHAPTER 2

The Perfection of Kindness: Soups

They've been thus my constant
enemy for a very long time;
And are the one single cause
that feeds and nourishes
The entire mass of harmful things.

How could I ever be free of all the terrors
Of cyclic life, and feel gladness so long as
They are rooted and fixed in my very heart?

I should therefore never turn back
Even for a single moment from the task
Of destroying the mental afflictions.

It is explained that the perfection
[Of kindness] consists of
Attaining a way of thinking wherein
One wishes to abandon [anything
that is harmful to others].

Master Shantideva, *Guide to the
Bodhisattva's Way of Life*

Contemplation:
1. See yourself blanketing all helpless and suffering beings with your compassion and kindness.
2. Bring them all under the protection of your equanimity.
3. Imagine that because of your goodness, they come to understand a gentler, more serene way of living.
4. Visualize a world of peace as a direct result of the peace you are cultivating in your own heart.

THE PERFECTION OF KINDNESS IS EMBODIED by moving through life with a perpetual goal never to disturb the calm, clear lake of the mind or heart of another being. We can stay in a state of high morality and live an ethical lifestyle by developing a razor-sharp sense of what is right and wrong for us, in our deepest heart. We can avoid saying and doing the things to ourselves and to others that keep us up at night and rob us of our peace. We can learn to recognize exactly what is the right thing to do.

I often think of a fellow student of our teachers' who shared a lovely story of the right thing to do.

While shopping at the supermarket for apples (or maybe it was oranges) he caught himself rummaging through the bin trying to find the most perfect, blemish-free fruit. So he consciously decided that he would find and buy only the blemished ones that were still fine to eat, inform the store manager of the rotten ones that were no longer good to eat and leave all the perfect ones for others.

The most profound level of kindness is to understand beyond the shadow of a doubt that by starting with the "man (or woman) in the mirror" we can and will eliminate all the suffering in the world and bring all beings to a state of peace.

I'm starting with the man in the mirror,

I'm asking him to change his ways.

No message could've been any clearer –

If you want to make the world a better place,

Take a look at yourself and then make the change.

Got to get it right while you've got the time,

Cause if you close your heart, then you close your mind.

Man in the Mirror, written by Siedah Garrett and Glen Ballard, performed by Michael Jackson on *Bad*

Bodhisattvas who have perfected kindness tread very gently in their world. They never harm any living being—in fact, they go to excruciating lengths to care for them. They are gentle; their hearts are wide open, giving comfort. They are kind—a concentrated source of goodness and nourishment for our souls—just as soups are to our bodies. Soups are the most easily digested and assimilated of foods. They are ideal in retreat when intense practice can decrease the appetite and slow down digestive and other processes. They are like the Bodhisattvas who have perfected morality and defeated the enemy of their own mental afflictions and take care of others with a tender compassion that can only come from the highest ethical standards and a selfless and intense desire to serve others. Church soup kitchens come to mind.

This level of care goes beyond empathy and compassion. It goes beyond teaching others to care for themselves. It extends to the direct perception that we have created all the beings that are suffering and we need to care for them, with the understanding that we are forced to witness in our world the results of "the enemy"—our own past harmful actions. If we really want to change our world and if we really care about the suffering we see, we will stop creating the causes to see it—the Man in the Mirror.

Sometimes we feel a massive burden lift from our hearts at this realization. We see that we are not helpless to do anything about the pain of the world. Wars, famine, disease, sexual abuse of children, racial and religious discrimination—all of it is changeable. A glimmer of hope, a ray of light begins to blaze, focused like a searchlight in a storm, seeking out the faces of each and every living being. We are filled with an intense desire to take care of them all.

PARADISE PUMPKIN SOUP

Serves 4–6

Soups lend themselves well to the Ayurvedic principles of combining the different tastes of sweet, sour, pungent, and salty. It is a very subtle and skilled art and we are trying to learn it. The combination of pumpkin (sweet) with ginger (pungent) and coconut oil (sweet) is marvelous.

¼ cup (60 ml) raw unrefined coconut oil
½ medium-sized ripe pumpkin, peeled and chopped into bite-sized chunks
1 leek, chopped
2 cups (500 ml) vegetable stock

1 tsp (5 ml) freshly chopped ginger
1 tsp (5 ml) chopped fresh thyme or
1/2 tsp (2.5 ml) dried thyme
sea salt and pepper, to taste

Heat oil in a large pot. Add the pumpkin chunks and the chopped leek. Sauté until brown.

Add the vegetable stock, ginger, thyme, salt, and pepper. Boil until pumpkin is very tender. Cream the soup with a hand-held blender or use a potato masher if this is not available. Re-season to taste. Serve as is, or with a splash of cream and lemon juice.

VEGETABLE MÉLANGE SOUP

Serves 4–6

We usually ended up making soups on Wednesday mornings. It was the perfect way to make room in our vegetable drawer for our SPUD delivery on Wednesday afternoons. We found that soups do not lend themselves well to quantification for recipe writing purposes! Basically, whatever we've had left went in the pot! Here's an example. Use any quantity of whatever vegetables you have on hand.

3 tbsp (45 ml) butter or coconut oil
1 tsp (5 ml) turmeric
1 tbsp (15 ml) coriander seeds
½ tsp (2.5 ml) mustard seeds
1 bell pepper, sliced
6–8 mushrooms, sliced
2–3 stalks celery, sliced
2–3 green onions
1 tbsp (15 ml) freshly grated ginger
2 carrots, chopped
¼ head cabbage, chopped
½ cup (125 ml) chopped squash
½ zucchini, sliced
5–6 cups (1.25 L – 1.5 L) water
sea salt and pepper, to taste.

Fry the spices in butter until fragrant. Add the bell pepper, mushrooms, celery, green onions, and ginger. Continue to fry until soft and browned. Add the rest of the vegetables and water. Simmer at low heat until liquid reduces somewhat. Add sea salt and pepper to taste. Now taste your soup. Adjust your seasonings as desired.

 Strain this soup to get a delicious clear vegetable stock that you can use in many other recipes. Can be frozen in resealable plastic bags.

LADA'S BEET BORSCHT

Our dear friend Lada's mother puts chopped tomatoes as well as tomato paste in her borscht, and her cousin adds a teaspoon of sugar just before serving. We preferred it with neither, but you can try both. I have a vision of beet borscht being a family undertaking. Enjoying relaxed family meals as often as you can is a crucial component of good digestion and assimilation of nutrients.

1 Tbsp (15 mL) butter
1 leek, sliced
3 medium beets, peeled and shredded
3 carrots, peeled and shredded
3 medium potatoes, peeled and cubed
5 cups (1.25 L) vegetable stock
½ medium head of cabbage, shredded
sea salt and pepper, to taste
½ cup (125 mL) sour cream (for garnish)
fresh dill, chopped
fresh parsley, chopped

Heat the butter in a skillet. Add the leek and sauté until translucent. Add the beets and carrots, and cook until tender. Set aside.

Boil the potatoes in the vegetable stock until they are about halfway done. Add the cooked vegetables and shredded cabbage, and cook until the cabbage is tender, about 15–20 minutes. Cover and turn off the heat. Let stand for 5 minutes.

Season to taste with salt and pepper. Delicious served with a garnish of sour cream, dill, and parsley.

This powerhouse combination soothes the soul, nourishes the body systems, and tantalizes the taste buds!

1 large squash, baked (any variety except pumpkin)
2 sweet potatoes, baked (the kind that are yellow inside are best)
2 cups (500 ml) vegetable stock or water
2 tbsp (30 ml) butter or coconut oil
1 tsp (5 ml) cumin seeds
¼ tsp (1 ml) white mustard seeds

pinch of fennel seeds
pinch of fenugreek seeds
2 stalks celery, very thinly sliced
1 green onion, thinly sliced
2 tbsp (30 ml) cream (optional)
sea salt and pepper, to taste

Remove the squash seeds and scoop out the flesh into a food processor. Halve the sweet potatoes and scoop out the flesh into the food processor. Add ½ cup (125 ml) of the vegetable stock or water and process until creamy and smooth. Transfer this to a saucepan and add the rest of the vegetable stock or water.

In a separate small fry pan, heat the butter and add the spices, allowing them to sizzle until fragrant but not burned. Lower the heat, add the celery and green onions, and sauté until slightly browned. Add this mixture to the soup.

Add the cream, if you like, season with salt and pepper, and reheat over low heat.

23

CURRIED ROAST VEGETABLE SOUP

SERVES 6-8

Curry powders and masalas (combinations of dried spices) are invaluable in the soup kitchen. They can add delicate or robust flavours to soups, providing an endless variety of tastes and ways to enjoy them. It's very similar to the kindness of the Bodhisattva, who has an infinite variety of tools in his/her toolbox—all ways to be of service to others and give them comfort, enjoyment, and love.

1 cup (250 ml) Japanese eggplant or any eggplant, chopped
sea salt, to taste
4 medium tomatoes, quartered
1 medium red bell pepper, cut in strips
1 medium green bell pepper, cut in strips
½ cup (125 ml) butter
2 leeks
1 tbsp (15 ml) jalapeño peppers, fresh or pickled, finely chopped

1 ½ tbsp (22.5 ml) ginger, freshly grated
1½ tsp (7.5 ml) curry powder
1 tsp (5 ml) ground cumin
1 tsp (5 ml) ground coriander
¼ tsp (1 ml) ground fenugreek
¼ tsp (1 ml) chilli powder
4 cups (1 L) vegetable stock
sea salt and pepper, to taste
¼ cup (60 ml) coconut milk
2 tbsp (30 ml) fresh herbs, chopped (for garnish)

Toss the eggplant with sea salt and let stand in a bowl for about an hour. This removes its bitter juice.

Roast the eggplant, tomatoes, and peppers in ¼ cup (60 ml) of the butter in a toaster oven until soft and browned, turning and basting with more butter as required. Set aside.

Brown the remaining butter in a saucepan over medium heat and add the leeks, jalapeño peppers, and ginger. Stir-fry for about 5 minutes until the leeks are soft. Add the curry powder, cumin, coriander, fenugreek, and chilli powder. Cook, stirring for 2 more minutes. Stir the roasted vegetables into the spice mixture and cook for several more minutes.

Add the stock and bring to a boil. Season with salt and pepper, reduce the heat and simmer uncovered for 10 minutes. Purée half of the soup and return it to the pot. Add the coconut milk and allow everything to simmer for another minute or two. Serve with a garnish of fresh herbs.

CHAPTER 3

The Perfection of Patience:
Cereals, Grains, Breads

It would be a complete impossibility
Ever to destroy altogether those
Irritating people, vast as space.
But the destruction of a single object,
The thought of anger
[In our own minds and hearts] is comparable
To destroying each and every enemy.
How could you ever find enough leather
To cover the entire surface of Earth?
Covering simply the soles of your feet
Is comparable to the entire surface.
If you hold to the sharp pain
Of thoughts like anger, your mind
Can know no peace;
You find no happiness,
No pleasure.
Sleep stays away,
And the mind remains unsettled.
Anger feeds on the food of feeling
upset, then strengthened
Turns to smash me. And so then I will smash
The sustenance that feeds
This enemy of mine.
My foe knows no other
Kind of work at all

Except to cause me pain.
No matter what happens
I will never allow
My joy to be disturbed.
Feeling upset cannot accomplish
My hopes, and only makes me lose
The goodness that I have.
There is nothing in the world
Which does not come easily
If you make a habit of it.
Make then a habit
Of bearing the small pains,
And thus endure the greater.

Master Shantideva, *Guide to the Bodhisattva's Way of Life*

Contemplation:
1. Recall a person toward whom you may be holding resentment or anger.
2. Recognize that this holding only serves to toxify you, mentally and physically, and performs no useful or productive function.
3. Imagine that the release of this poison of anger from your own heart sweeps across the planet as a vast rainbow of love.

BY EXERCISING OUR SELF-DISCIPLINE AND controlling our emotions when the going gets tough, we learn the Perfection of Patience. We must learn and habituate ourselves to alternative reactions to supplant our deep seeds for impulsive, almost reflexive outbursts of anger when our most sensitive buttons are being jumped on. We can cultivate a mind that has the priceless ability to be the watcher of the thought process rather than the thinker.

Master Shantideva calls it being like a "bump on a log" when the anger hits. We strive for a mind that has stepped away from identifying itself with harmful or afflictive emotions, and has trained itself to view them as clouds simply moving across an otherwise completely clear sky. The bright sun of the perfection of patience can eventually permanently vaporize these clouds.

Master Shantideva says that all our anger is initially triggered by getting upset. This throws us off balance, which only feeds our anger.

> If there is something you can
> do about it, why feel upset?
> If there is nothing you can do about
> it, what use is being upset?
>
> Master Shantideva, *Guide to the
> Bodhisattva's Way of Life*

Ultimately we come to the understanding that we could never experience anger unless we had caused anger to others. Just the same as the experience of tasty or repulsive food! We are the cause for all of our experiences.

Perfect patience is a mental habit. Like any other habit, with practice it can be cultivated and developed. Master Shantideva's advises us to start by practicing with small pains—things like feeling too hot, or too cold, or staying unperturbed when someone makes an incendiary remark, or provokes us. True patience is the ability to stay cool when the anger rises, not when the bread doesn't.

SERVES 4–6

For the highest benefit and best assimilation, soak all whole grains in water, yogurt, and/or buttermilk for 12–24 hours before cooking. The results are simply delicious! Oats, like rye, barley, and especially wheat contain gluten and should be consumed only after being soaked or fermented. This breaks down the gluten and other proteins that are not easily digested. If you don't soak your oats, the chronic stress on the digestive mechanisms can eventually manifest as allergies, celiac disease, mental illness, chronic indigestion, and yeast infections.

1 cup (250 ml) rolled or cracked oats
2 tbsp (30 ml) yogurt
½ tsp (2.5 ml) sea salt
1 cup (250 ml) almond milk

grating of nutmeg
grating of fresh ginger
¼ tsp (1 ml) cardamom
¼ tsp (1 ml) cinnamon

28

In a large bowl, mix the oats with 1 cup (250 ml) warm water, yogurt, and salt. Cover and leave in a warm place for 12–24 hours.

In a small saucepan, bring the almond milk to a boil. Add the soaked oats and spices, reduce the heat, cover and simmer for about 5 minutes.

Serve this dish with plenty of cream and a drizzle of raw honey or maple syrup. Mashed dates, prunes and bananas also go well.

COCONUT SUGAR AND LIME FRENCH TOAST

SERVES 4

My son Jordan and his partner Miriam served us this classic with the delicious twist of lime juice. It was a long time ago, and I've never forgotten it. I replaced the brown sugar from their original dish with coconut sugar, which has a lovely subtle flavour. It's also great with maple syrup mixed with lime juice. Experiment with different kinds of bread for your favourite texture and mouth feel. If you use coarser, denser breads such as whole wheat or sprouted wheat as we did, it's best to soak the bread slices in the egg mixture for a while.

2 tbsp (30 ml) butter, more for spreading

4 eggs

½ cup (125 ml) whole milk

½ tsp (2.5 ml) cinnamon

tiny pinch ground cardamom (optional)

8 slices of bread

½ cup (125 ml) coconut sugar

2 limes, juiced

Melt the butter in a fry pan on high.

Beat eggs, milk, cinnamon, and cardamom in a bowl. Soak each piece of bread in the mixture and then transfer immediately into the fry pan. Reduce heat to medium, turn when the edges are crispy and browned.

As you remove the bread slices, spread a little butter, 1 tbsp (15 ml) of coconut sugar, and 1 ½ tsp (7.5 ml) lime juice on each slice. Serve immediately.

LAKSHMI'S GRANOLA

Our friend Lakshmi sent us this amazing concoction by parcel post when we had been in deep retreat for a year or so. It's really extraordinary soaked overnight in yogurt, milk, or cream.

1 cup (250 ml) mixed nuts
1 cup (250 ml) organic coconut milk
¼ cup (60 ml) maple syrup
½ cup (125 ml) hemp hearts
2 tbsp (30 ml) unground flax seeds
3 tbsp (45 ml) ground flax seeds
½ cup (125 ml) chopped mixed dried fruit
¼ cup (60 ml) butter
2 tbsp (30 ml) cinnamon

¼ cup (60 ml) honey
5 cloves, ground
1½ inch (4 cm) vanilla bean, ground or
1 tsp (5 ml) pure vanilla essence
¼ tsp (1 ml) coarse sea salt
½ tsp (2.5 ml) ground cardamom
5 cups (1.25 L) rolled or quick oats
1 tsp (5 ml) freshly grated ginger

Prepare the mixed nuts ahead of time by soaking in salt water overnight, then toasting at 170°F (77°C) for 8–12 hours. (Cashews only require a 6-hour soak.)

Preheat oven to 300°F (150°C). In a saucepan, simmer coconut milk and maple syrup until it reduces to the consistency of sweet condensed milk. This should take about 40 minutes. Allow to cool.

In a bowl, mix together the hemp hearts, unground and ground flax seeds, soaked nuts, and dried fruit.

Melt the butter in a small saucepan and remove from heat. Mix in the cinnamon, honey, ground cloves, vanilla, salt, and cardamom. Mix three-quarters of the butter mixture with the oats and ginger. Spread this on a baking sheet and toast for 20 minutes. Stir well then toast for another 20–30 minutes. Allow to cool.

Mix the remaining butter mixture with the hemp heart mixture, and finally combine everything together—the coconut-milk mixture, hemp-heart-plus-butter mixture, and the toasted-oats mixture.

Lakshmi says to store this granola in a refrigerator if you don't think it will be enjoyed within the month!

JIKJETTE WARM QUINOA AND SPINACH SALAD

SERVES 8–10

Jikjette is another nickname for our friend Madhuri. She introduced us to this comforting dish, and there's a secret unlisted ingredient that she always adds—love.

½ tsp (2.5 ml) pink Himalayan rock salt
1 cup (250 ml) uncooked quinoa
3 cups (750 ml) fresh spinach, chopped
2 carrots, peeled and grated
1/3 cup (80 ml) almonds, toasted
and coarsely chopped

2 tbsp (30 ml) chopped cilantro
2 tbsp (30 ml) extra-virgin olive oil
1 tbsp (15 ml) agave or maple syrup (optional)
juice of ½ lime
pinch of cayenne (optional)
sea salt, to taste

Salt 2 cups (500 ml) of water with the Himalayan rock salt. Soak the quinoa in the salted water overnight, then drain well. Bring quinoa to a boil in 2 cups (500 ml) water. Reduce heat to a simmer and cook covered for about 10 minutes, or until the eyes of the quinoa grains emerge. Fluff with a fork and cool for about 15–20 minutes. Add the remaining ingredients and toss until thoroughly mixed. The warmer the quinoa, the more the spinach will be wilted. Add additional salt to taste and serve.

You can cook the quinoa in vegetable broth instead of water for added flavour. This recipe is great with grilled tempeh, smoked tofu, or tossed with 1/4 cup crumbled goat cheese.

BUCKWHEAT PANCAKE STACK WITH
BLACKBERRY-ORANGE SYRUP

SERVES 6–8

Buckwheat is not a grain; it's a fruit. Like rice, millet, and quinoa, it doesn't contain gluten, making it more digestible than wheat, oats, rye, and barley. Amaranth, kamut, and spelt are other options for very tasty grains that may be easier to digest than wheat. All are best pre-soaked for 12–24 hours in yogurt and water or lemon water. Buckwheat gives us all eight essential amino acids and is a rich source of lysine and calcium as well as vitamin E and the entire B-complex group, especially nitriloside, B-17, said to defend against cancer. This recipe pairs it with whole wheat, which is deficient in lysine.

FOR THE BUCKWHEAT PANCAKES:

½ cup (125 ml) buckwheat flour
½ cup (125 ml) whole-wheat flour
1 cup (250 ml) buttermilk or yogurt,
or ½ cup (125 ml) of each

1 egg, beaten
1½ tsp (7.5 ml) molasses (optional)
½ tsp (2.5 ml) baking soda
1 tbsp (15 ml) butter

FOR THE BLACKBERRY-ORANGE SYRUP:

2 cups (500 ml) wild blackberries or other berries
zest of 1 orange

juice of 1 orange
maple syrup, to taste

FOR THE BUCKWHEAT PANCAKES:

Soak the flours in the yogurt and/or buttermilk for 24 hours in a warm place, covered with a cloth.

Gently beat in egg, molasses, and baking soda.

In a small fry pan, melt butter until browned on medium-low heat and pour in the batter to desired size of pancake. Top will begin to bubble when ready to flip. Flip and cook until underside is browned.

FOR THE BLACKBERRY-ORANGE SYRUP:

Bring blackberries, orange zest, and orange juice to a boil, reduce heat and simmer gently for 45 minutes to an hour or until liquid has reduced and consistency becomes syrupy. Add maple syrup to taste.

♡ These pancakes will take a bit longer than conventional pancakes to cook, but are well worth the time. Serve with butter and blackberry-orange syrup or raw honey.

DATE-WALNUT BREAD

This recipe is modified from some of Sally Fallon's bread recipes in *Nourishing Traditions*. None of them use white flour, white sugar, or baking powder. They all use nuts, soaked whole-wheat flour, and a very small amount of sweetener in the form of maple syrup and/or dried fruit. Their moistness and distinct lack of the heaviness that usually characterizes 100% whole-wheat baking will amaze you!

Dates impart their sweetness and moistness to this bread as well as their abundance of potassium. Walnuts were used traditionally as a home remedy for the kidneys and lungs and to lubricate the large intestine. If your walnuts taste bitter, they have become rancid. Always store them in the refrigerator.

1 cup (250 ml) crispy walnuts
3 cups (750 ml) freshly stone-
ground whole-wheat flour
2 cups (500 ml) buttermilk
2 cups (500 ml) dates, pitted
½ cup (125 ml) butter, melted

3 eggs, beaten
1 tbsp (15 ml) maple syrup
2 tsp (10 ml) baking soda
1 tsp (5 ml) pure vanilla essence
1 tsp (5 ml) sea salt

Soak the walnuts in salt water for 12–24 hours, then drain and toast at 175°F (80°C) for 8–12 hours. Soak flour in buttermilk for 12–24 hours, covered with a towel, in a warm place. Bread rises better if the flour is soaked for 24 hours.

Preheat oven to 325°F (160°C). Boil the pitted dates with a little water until soft, then mash. Blend the buttermilk/flour mixture with all the remaining ingredients. Pour into a generously buttered loaf pan and bake for 20–30 minutes, or until a toothpick inserted into the middle comes out clean.

 These are easy to eat and freeze if baked in muffin tins instead of a loaf pan
Use this recipe and preparation method, but substitute the fruit and nuts for these yummy variations:

- Apricot-Almond Bread. Almonds offer the highest source of calcium and fibre of all nuts and seeds and contain potential cancer inhibitors. Dried apricots gift us with beta carotene, fibre, copper, and cobalt. Use: 2 cups (500 ml) dried apricots, chopped, soaked in boiling water until soft, then drained and 1 cup (250 ml) crispy almonds.
- Banana-Pecan Bread. Bananas are super rich sources of potassium. Pecans fortify us with their abundant iron, calcium, phosphorus, and potassium. Use: 2 ripe bananas, mashed and 1 cup (250 ml) crispy pecans.

WHOLE-WHEAT NAAN

SERVES 6–8

Wheat is a great source of protein but is deficient in lysine, so it's best to eat other proteins with whole-wheat breads (eggs, cheese, lentils, or nut butters form complete proteins in combination with whole wheat).

If whole wheat is grown in fertile soil, it provides abundant B vitamins, calcium, and iron. It's crucial that the wheat is milled at a low temperature to keep the nutrients intact and prevent its high quality omega-3 linolenic acid from going rancid.

3 tbsp (45 ml) yogurt
1 cup (250 ml) whole-wheat flour
1 tsp (5 ml) fresh yeast
1 tsp (5 ml) coconut sugar
¼ cup (60 ml) warm water
1 tsp (5 ml) sea salt
1 tbsp (15 ml) ghee or melted butter
unbleached white flour, for kneading
¼ cup (60 ml) butter

Mix the yogurt with ¼ cup (60 ml) of water. Soak the whole-wheat flour in the yogurt-water mixture, covered with a towel, for 12–24 hours in a warm place.

Put the yeast and sugar in a cup with the warm water, mix well until yeast has dissolved and set aside in a warm place for 10 minutes until mixture starts to froth.

Place the soaked flour in a large mixing bowl and add the salt. Make a well in the middle, add the tablespoon of ghee and pour in the yeast mixture. Mix well with hands to form dough, adding more water if required.

Turn the dough onto a floured surface and knead for about 5 minutes or until smooth. Place the dough back in the bowl, cover and let rise in a warm place for 1½ hours or until doubled in bulk.

Preheat oven to broil. Turn the dough onto a floured surface and knead for 2 minutes. Break off small balls, pat into rounds about 5 inches (12 cm) in diameter and ½-inch (1 cm) thick. Place on a buttered sheet of tinfoil and place under a very hot preheated broiler for 7–10 minutes, turning twice and basting with butter. Serve warm immediately or keep wrapped in foil until ready to serve.

MILLET CAKES

SERVES 10–12

Millet is a high-quality protein packed with nutrition. It's rich in B vitamins and lysine, which is lacking in wheat. Millet also contains no gluten, which is the protein in wheat that many of us find difficult to digest. Millet is very low in phytates so it isn't necessary to pre-soak it.

2 cups (500 ml) uncooked millet
2 eggs, beaten
¼ cup (60 ml) unbleached white flour
½ tsp (2.5 ml) sea salt
1/8 tsp (0.5 ml) pepper
1/8 tsp (0.5 ml) cayenne pepper

2 green onions, finely sliced
½ bunch cilantro, chopped
½ cup (125 ml) grated Parmesan cheese
2 tbsp (30 ml) butter
2 tbsp (30 ml) olive oil

Bring 5 cups (1.25 L) of water to a rolling boil, add the millet, reduce heat, and simmer for 30 minutes. Leave the millet draining in a sieve while you prepare the rest of the ingredients.

Blend the beaten eggs with the flour and seasonings and fold in the cooked millet, green onions, cilantro, and cheese. Form the mixture into patties.

Melt the butter with the olive oil in a fry pan on medium heat. Sauté the patties. When air bubbles form on the patties and the edges start to crisp, turn to cook the other side.

AMARANTH AND KAMUT PILAF

Kamut and amaranth have distinctive, nutty flavours and textures and provide us with abundant and superior proteins. Kamut has 30% more protein than wheat and is rich in magnesium, zinc, and vitamin E. Amaranth gives us 60 mg of calcium per half cup! Soak both for 12–24 hours in yogurt or buttermilk to neutralize any enzyme inhibitors and make them far easier to digest and enjoy.

½ cup (125 ml) amaranth
½ cup (125 ml) kamut
1 cup (250 ml) yogurt
½ cup (125 ml) raisins
2 tbsp (30 ml) butter
1 tsp (5 ml) coriander seeds
½ tsp (2.5 ml) cumin seeds

½ tsp (2.5 ml) turmeric
½ tsp (2.5 ml) cinnamon
½ cup (125 ml) julienned bell peppers
(red, green, yellow, or a combination)
½ cup (125 ml) almonds, sliced and toasted
2 tbsp (30 ml) cilantro, chopped

Combine the amaranth, kamut, and yogurt in a medium-sized bowl. Add a little water to cover the grains. Soak the grains for 24 hours, covered with a towel, in a warm place.

Pour the soaked grains into a pot, add 3 cups (750 ml) water and bring to a rolling boil. Cover and reduce heat to simmer for about 1 hour or more, until kernels are tender but still chewy. Remove from heat, mix in the raisins, and set aside.

Melt the butter in a fry pan. Fry the coriander and cumin seeds with the turmeric and cinnamon in the butter on low heat until fragrant. Add the peppers and continue frying until peppers are tender. Add the grains and toss with the spices and peppers. Toss in the almonds and cilantro and serve immediately. Serve immediately.

38

QUINOA TABBOULEH

This recipe uses quinoa instead of the traditional bulgur wheat. Quinoa offers us twice the protein of corn or rice. It has 16–20% ideal quality protein with high levels of cysteine, lysine, and methionine; amino acids that tend to be low in other grains. Peruvian mothers eat quinoa to stimulate the flow of breast milk. Quinoa contains more iron, phosphorus, calcium, and vitamins A, E, and B than other grains. It does contain some anti-nutrients which can be difficult to digest (saponins, phytates, and lectins) and should be pre-soaked for 12 hours in water with a little yogurt or lemon juice prior to cooking.

½ cup (125 ml) quinoa
1 cup (250 ml) vegetable broth
¼ cup (60 ml) extra-virgin olive oil
3 tbsp (45 ml) chopped mint
1 tomato, chopped

1 bunch parsley, chopped
2 stalks celery, finely sliced
1 clove garlic (optional)
3 green onions, thinly sliced
juice of 1 lemon

Bring quinoa to a boil in vegetable broth. Reduce heat to a simmer and cook covered for about 10 minutes, or until the eyes of the quinoa grains emerge. Transfer cooked quinoa into a large bowl. Fluff with a fork and cool for about 20 - 30 minutes. Combine with remaining ingredients.

39

LADA'S FALAFEL

We adapted this recipe slightly because we don't have a meat grinder, which our friend Lada used when she would serve this in her Mediterranean taverna, House of Taste. We also did a power soak using boiling water since we noticed a slight propensity to indigestion when we ate chickpeas. Adding lemon juice to induce fermentation and giving the chickpeas a long soak helped to alleviate this.

1 cup (250 ml) dried chickpeas
2 tbsp (30 ml) lemon juice, divided
2 cups (500 ml) fresh parsley
1 clove garlic (optional)
1 tsp (5 ml) coriander
½ tsp (2.5 ml) cumin
¼ tsp (1 ml) cayenne (optional)
½ tsp (2.5 ml) homemade baking powder (page XXIV)
sea salt and pepper, to taste
5 tbsp (75 ml) olive oil

Pour enough boiling water to cover the chickpeas. Stir in 1 tbsp (15 ml) of the lemon juice and leave in a warm place for 12 hours.

Pour off excess water and cover with fresh boiling water again and the remaining 1 tbsp (15 ml) of lemon juice. Leave in a warm place for another 12 hours.

Drain and grind in a food processor. Add the parsley and garlic. Keep processing. Sprinkle in the spices, baking powder, salt, pepper, and process further until ground enough to stick together but not totally smooth.

Form the dough into balls about the size of walnuts, slightly flattened. Fry in the oil at medium heat until golden brown, a few minutes on each side. Drain on paper towels.

Serve these falafels with Yogurt Cilantro Chutney (page 73) and Whole-Wheat Naan (page 36). They're also great with plain brown rice or stuffed into tortillas.

This recipe, from our friend Lali, helped give Diamond Forest the reputation of being the Five Diamond hotel of retreat centres. Not to mention the fact that spelt and kamut both contain 30% more protein than wheat. Spelt is abundantly generous with its B vitamins, magnesium, and fibre, and kamut with magnesium, zinc, and vitamin E. Both grains contain gluten but are tolerated well by many wheat-sensitive people.

For the salad:

½ cup (125 ml) kamut kernels
⅓ cup (125 ml) spelt kernels
2 tbsp (30 ml) yogurt
½ cup (125 ml) corn kernels, fresh or frozen

½ cup (125 ml) currants
½ red bell pepper, diced
2 tbsp (30 ml) sliced green onions
sea salt and pepper, to taste

For the dressing:

2 tbsp (30 ml) natural rice vinegar
1 tsp (5 ml) honey
½ tsp (2.5 ml) Dijon mustard
½ tsp (2.5 ml) sea salt
¼ tsp (1 ml) pepper

¼ cup (60 ml) olive oil
1 tbsp (15 ml) finely chopped shallot
1 tbsp (15 ml) chopped cilantro
1 tsp (5 ml) freshly grated ginger
For the salad:

Combine the kamut kernels, spelt kernels, and yogurt in a medium-sized bowl. Add a little water to cover the grains. Soak for 24 hours, covered, in a warm place.

In a medium saucepan, bring 4 cups (1 L) of water to a boil. Add soaked kamut and spelt kernels and bring to a boil again. Reduce heat to low, cover and simmer for about 45 minutes or until kernels are tender, but still chewy. Let kernels drain in a sieve for about 1½ hours or until they're at room temperature. Toss with the rest of the salad ingredients.

For the dressing:

In a small bowl, whisk together vinegar, honey, mustard, salt, and pepper. Gently whisk in the oil, shallot, cilantro, and ginger. Drizzle the vinaigrette over the grains and vegetables, toss to coat. Add salt and pepper to taste. Cover tightly and refrigerate overnight or until chilled.

CHAPTER 4

THE PERFECTION OF JOY IN MAKING GREAT EFFORT: MAIN COURSE MEALS

Once you have practiced patience,
Begin your practice of effort
For enlightenment lies in making
these kinds of effort.
Without a breeze they never flicker,
And just so in the absence of effort,
merit can never occur.
What is effort?
It is joy in doing good.

A single instance of clear mind
Can as a result lead you
To the Pure One or the like.

Along these same lines the related actions
Of body and speech are unable to give
A result if one's efforts are feeble.

Master Shantideva, *Guide to the
Bodhisattva's Way of Life*

Contemplation:

1. See yourself as a being that is beyond fatigue, fear, and a limited capacity. What would this feel like?

2. Recall a time when you had boundless energy and vitality.

3. Imagine that your ability to serve others knows no bounds and that you experience no human constraints.

4. Imagine yourself tirelessly, ecstatically doing whatever is necessary to bring joy and fulfillment to others.

THE ULTIMATE EXPRESSION OF WHAT ALL the great yogic masters call Karma Yoga (the yoga of activity) is the Perfection of Joy in Making Great Effort which, when perfected, automatically evolves into Bhakti Yoga (the yoga of devotion). It is a delicious and sublime sense of totally abandoning oneself into work or an activity that benefits many and holds no particular self-interest, other than the inevitable enlightened state that comes from serving others!

His Holiness the 14th Dalai Lama refers to this enlightened self-interest as the understanding that taking care of others and ensuring that no harm comes to them is the fastest way to one's own enlightenment. The essence of this joy is indescribable bliss.

> The total amount of happiness that exists in the world has come from wanting to make others happy. The total amount of suffering that exists in the world has come from wanting to make ourselves happy.
>
> Master Shantideva, *Guide to the Bodhisattva's Way of Life*

To fathom this at the deepest level is to perfect taking joy in making great effort.

This section is devoted to putting in the effort required to produce a truly delectable dish that is both nourishing and delicious. The key word here is joy. I am reminded of a story told by a dear friend who was one of the primary caretakers for our teachers when they did a great retreat of three years, three months, and three days from 2000–2003. She and another of the caretaker cooks had been arguing while preparing the evening meal for the retreatants. The next morning, the tray with the prior evening's food was untouched! My friend and her fellow caretakers made peace amongst themselves in time to prepare that day's dinner. The following morning, a short but loaded note accompanied the tray of dishes, this time empty and clean! The note read "Thank You".

Making great effort means not succumbing to the spiritual laziness that accompanies any mentally

afflicted state. We all have an innate tendency to blame others for our woes. It's much easier to dwell on the faults of others. But there comes a time when we realize that nothing has ever changed from waiting for someone else to change. It usually happens around the same time we notice how many different jobs, partners, and medical treatments we've been through. And that's usually when we start making great efforts with gusto to *cook with hot oil* in order to destroy our mental afflictions.

Our food is charged with the energy emitting from our hands and our souls as we prepare it. Feelings of anger, resentment, depression or other negative mind states become part of the pranic force of the food we prepare, and this pranic force transmits into all those who eat this food. On the other hand, if we prepare food with love, purity, happiness, and peace, this positive and beneficial energy will pour into those we feed and forms part of their prana.

Master Shantideva says it all depends on undertaking any activity with clear and focused concentration imbued with joy. It is in making the dreams of others come true that we experience the highest bliss.

Many of the following recipes require overnight soaking or multi-day sprouting operations ahead of time. I suggest you read through an entire recipe before deciding to make it, so you know what's coming! Set aside enough time for these recipes so that your meal preparation efforts are infused with a leisurely sense of enjoyment. We kept soaked and toasted nuts of every variety on hand, so that when we needed them, they were ready to go.

AVOCADO AND CASHEW-CREAM SOBA NOODLE PASTA

SERVES 4–6

Avocados are highly nutritious and delicious sources of goodness. They give us carotenoids, B and C vitamins, potassium, magnesium, iron, calcium, and phosphorus. Their mostly mono-unsaturated oleic acid is complete with lipase and vitamin E. Cashews, which are very rich in protein, also provide high amounts of magnesium, phosphorus, and potassium. Both avocados and nut creams gift us with an alternate source of creamy mouth feel to dairy creams. This textural quality of food is very important—both Master Swatmarama in the *Hatha Yoga Pradipika* and Sally Fallon refer to it often in their seminal texts.

1 leek, chopped
2 tbsp (30 ml) coconut oil
¾ cup (185 ml) baked, mashed squash
¾ cup (185 ml) cashew nuts, soaked for 4–6 hours
½ cup (125 ml) grated pecorino or
Parmesan cheese (optional)
1/3 cup (80 ml) olive oil

1/3 cup (80 ml) whipping cream (optional)
1 ripe avocado
2–3 small tomatoes
1 tsp (5 ml) lime juice, freshly squeezed
sea salt and pepper, to taste
½ lb (250 g) soba noodles (or your choice of noodles), cooked

Fry leeks in coconut oil until lightly browned, then blend with the rest of the ingredients (except the noodles) in a food processor until creamy and smooth. Heat gently over very low heat and serve over Japanese soba (buckwheat) noodles or noodles of your choice prepared according to package instructions.

KAREN'S NUT-BUTTER CURRY BEAN STEW

SERVES 4–6

This delicious stew from our friend Karen provides copious amounts of protein.

1 tbsp (15 ml) olive oil
1 large zucchini, diced
2 large carrots, diced
4 tomatoes, diced
2 tbsp (30 ml) peanut butter (organic, crunchy is best)
1½ cups (375 ml) cooked garbanzo beans,
1 tbsp (15 ml) curry powder, to taste
sea salt, to taste
1 bunch of spinach, separated

In a large soup pot, heat the oil, add the zucchini and carrots, and cook until tender. Add the tomatoes and a large dollop of peanut butter. Continue simmering until tomatoes break down. Add garbanzo beans, curry powder, and salt. Taste the stew and adjust seasonings. Add the head of spinach a few minutes before serving so the spinach stays bright green. Serve on a bed of brown rice.

♡ Garbanzo beans usually come in 375 – 425g cans which are convenient if you don't have the time to cook fresh ones. Be sure to drain and rinse them well.

FRENCH-BAKED AZUKI BEANS

Serves 4–6

This is a wild French recipe that calls for cooking the beans in olive oil, not water! We used azuki beans instead of small white beans, substituted leeks for the onions, omitted the garlic, and used Uncle Harvey's Tomato Sauce instead of tomato paste.

4 cups (1 L) azuki beans
¼ cup (60 ml) yogurt
1 cup (250 ml) extra-virgin olive oil
1 cup (250 ml) Uncle Harvey's
Tomato Sauce (page 69)

several sprigs fresh thyme, tied together
other chopped fresh or dried herbs of your choice
2 large leeks, thinly sliced
2 lemons, freshly squeezed
sea salt and pepper, to taste

49

Pour boiling water over the dried beans to cover, mix in the yogurt and leave covered in a warm place for 12 hours. Drain and rinse the beans.

Preheat oven to 300°F (150°C). Heat the olive oil in a large casserole pot. Add the beans, tomato sauce, and herbs. Bake for about 1½ hours, stirring often to prevent burning. If beans seem too dry, add more olive oil.

Test a bean occasionally for tenderness. They should be soft but not at all mushy. Remove the sprigs of thyme, fold in the sliced leeks and lemon juice, season to taste, and serve with brown rice or fresh bread.

MEXICAN CHEESY RICE CASSEROLE

SERVES 6–8

Because cheesy is the operative word here, and because this dish is VERY dairy-heavy, I only suggest making this dish if you have a high tolerance to dairy. We spaced our dairy-rich dishes out or often substituted nut creams for dairy if we found ourselves becoming overly phlegmy. Interestingly, we didn't always experience increased phlegm from large amounts of dairy.

Obviously the causes of phlegm aren't inherent in dairy products! But if we have created the causes for phlegm or congestion through harming others, then dairy products may be just the contributing factor we need to experience phlegm ourselves. Armed with this awareness, and with a solid intention to avoid harming others in these ways, we can overcome these types of food intolerances and other negative karmic influences and slowly evolve into Peacock Bodhisattvas.

1½ cups (375 ml) grated cheese (cheddar, Gouda, Edam, Asiago, or your choice), divided
4 cups (1 L) cooked brown rice
2 large leeks, sliced
½ cup (125 ml) black olives, pitted and sliced
1 cup (250 ml) sour cream
2–3 pickled jalapeño peppers, finely chopped

Preheat oven to 350°F (180°C). Set aside ½ cup (125 ml) of the grated cheese. Combine the rest of the ingredients and pour into a buttered baking casserole dish. Top with the reserved cheese and bake for about half an hour.

SESAME CRUSTED TOFU WITH SPICY ALMOND SAUCE

SERVES 4–6

In Japan, tofu is widely consumed, but always in very small amounts—as a side dish, condiment, or in miso soup. I recommend adopting these guidelines for enjoying tofu. Eating any more than a few pieces always caused us gastric distress, which was greatly mitigated if we ate some ginger or fermented food, like miso, or fermented vegetables, like tsukemono, with our tofu.

Put the tofu, sesame seeds, ginger, flour, red pepper flakes, and sea salt in a large re-sealable plastic bag and shake gently until the tofu pieces are well coated. Set aside while you make the spicy almond sauce.

In a small saucepan, combine almond butter, curry paste, coconut milk, ketchup, soy sauce, and simmer very gently on low heat, beating constantly with a whisk, until smooth and creamy. Add hot water if it appears too thick.

Heat the coconut oil and butter in a fry pan. Fry the tofu until browned and crispy on the outside. Drain on paper towels. Serve on a bowl of brown rice, rice noodles. or in tortilla wraps covered with the sauce.

¼ lb (125 g) organic medium-firm tofu, rinsed in cold water and chopped into bite-size rectangles
3 tbsp (45 ml) white or black sesame seeds, toasted
1 tbsp (15 ml) freshly grated ginger
1 tbsp (15 ml) unbleached white flour
½ tsp (2.5 ml) red pepper flakes
½ tsp (2.5 ml) sea salt
¼ cup (60 ml) almond butter
1 tsp (5 ml) Thai curry paste
½ cup (125 ml) coconut milk
1 tbsp (15 ml) organic ketchup
1 tsp (5 ml) soy sauce
3 tbsp (45 ml) coconut oil
1 tsp (5 ml) butter

MADHURI'S COCONUT-GINGER KITCHARI

SERVES 6–8

Kitchari is a Sanskrit word meaning food of the Gods. There is a certain skill to imparting subtlety or robustness to food as opposed to blandness or harshness—our friend Madhuri is a master at harmonizing flavours, textures, and fragrances. She has a theory that Ayurvedically balanced foods—by spice, taste, quality, and presentation/preparation—help the inner body ease and slide back into place. She calls this a "bindu balancing stew".

52

1 cup (250 ml) uncooked rice
1 cup (250 ml) mung dal or dried lentils
3 tbsp (45 ml) lemon juice or apple cider vinegar
2 tbsp (30 ml) ghee
2 tbsp (30 ml) freshly grated ginger
2 cups (500 ml) cubed carrots
1 cup (250 ml) chopped celery
2 tbsp (30 ml) tridoshic spice blend (page 68)

one 12 oz (355 ml) can coconut milk
6 cups (1.5 L) water, fresh and filtered
1 tbsp (15 ml) sea salt
1 cup (250 ml) cubed zucchini
2/3 cup (160 ml) chopped cilantro, divided
1 lime (optional)
plain yogurt (optional)

Pre-soak rice and mung dal with a pinch of salt and lemon juice or apple cider vinegar in enough water to cover. Soak overnight or up to 24 hours. Remember to rinse and replace with fresh water once a day, if you are soaking more than overnight. Rinse and strain well.

Heat a large pot on medium and add ghee when warm. Lightly sauté ginger until fragrant. Add the carrots, celery, and tridoshic spice blend, stirring frequently to keep the spices from burning while allowing the flavours to be released. The mixture should be sizzling but not burning or sticking to the bottom of the pan. Stir in rice and dal. Sauté for another minute or two. Pour in the coconut milk and bring to a light boil. Add the water and salt. Bring kitchari mixture to a boil, cover and turn down to a vigorous simmer, stirring occasionally until everything is cooked down into a soft, stew-like consistency. "Give it some love and let it simmer," says Madhuri. This should take approximately 45–60 minutes.

When the kitchari is almost done, stir in zucchini and half of the chopped cilantro, so they don't end up overcooked. Let the kitchari rest in the pot for about 10–15 minutes prior to serving. Garnish with a squeeze of lime juice, dollop of plain yogurt, and the remaining fresh cilantro.

MASOOR DAL (RED LENTILS)

This is a lovely basic dal recipe made with lemon juice. Red lentils cook quickly and while it isn't absolutely necessary to soak them, we still gave them a soak for several hours prior to cooking.

2 tbsp (30 ml) yogurt
1 cup (250 ml) red lentils
4 curry leaves
½ tsp (2.5 ml) freshly grated ginger
¼ tsp (1 ml) chilli powder
¼ tsp (1 ml) turmeric
1 tsp (5 ml) sea salt

2 tomatoes, cut into chunks
2 tbsp (30 ml) lemon juice
2 tbsp (30 ml) chopped cilantro
2 tbsp (30 ml) ghee
½ tsp (2.5 ml) cumin seeds
1 diced red chilli (optional)

Combine 2 cups (500 ml) of water with the yogurt. Soak the lentils in the water-yogurt mixture for several hours. Rinse well and drain.

In a large saucepan, combine the soaked lentils with 3 cups (750 ml) of water and the curry leaves, ginger, chilli powder, and turmeric. Simmer, covered, for 20–25 minutes until most of the water has evaporated and the lentils are soft enough to be mashed. Remove from heat and mash. Add the salt, tomatoes, lemon juice, cilantro, and another 1 cup (250 ml) of water. Cook over medium heat for about 5 minutes, stirring. Remove from heat and set aside.

Heat the ghee in a pan and add the cumin seeds and diced red chilli. When the seeds turn a shade darker, remove from heat and let stand for a bit before pouring over the lentils. Serve immediately.

BUCKWHEAT KASHA CASSEROLE

SERVES 8–10

This recipe is a good contender for the *Perfection of Patience* section as well as the *Perfection of Joy in Making Great Effort* section! Relax and enjoy the process. The result is delicious.

1 cup (250 ml) whole raw buckwheat groats (kasha)
2 tbsp (30 ml) yogurt
1 large leek, chopped
2 tbsp (30 ml) butter
2 tbsp (30 ml) olive oil
1½ cups (375 ml) sliced potato
sea salt and pepper, to taste
1 cup (250 ml) vegetable stock

Sprout the raw buckwheat groats by filling glass jars one-third full with the kasha. Add 1½ cups (375 ml) water per jar and cover with mesh or cheesecloth. Allow to soak overnight, then drain and rinse the grains well. Invert the jars and let sit at an angle on a dish rack so it can continue to drain and allow air to circulate. Rinse and repeat 2–3 times per day for about 2 days or until tiny sprouts appear. This method of sprouting is the same for all grains and seeds. The only difference is how long it takes for the grains to sprout. If they don't sprout, it means they have been irradiated—best not to eat them.

Once sprouts appear, drain well, spread out on a baking sheet and bake at 150°F (65°C) overnight or until grains are totally dried. Store in airtight jars in the refrigerator.

Now that the kasha has been sprouted, it doesn't require further soaking before cooking unless you want to ferment it, which we often did. To ferment the kasha, fry the sprouted buckwheat groats over medium heat in a cast-iron or stainless steel fry pan with a lid, shaking occasionally. Remove from heat, mix with 1½ cups (375 ml) water and the yogurt, cover and let stand in a warm place for at least 7 hours.

Preheat oven to 350°F (180°C). Sauté the chopped leek in butter and olive oil, then add the potatoes, salt, and pepper. Sauté until the potatoes are lightly browned. Add the potatoes, vegetable stock, and buckwheat to a casserole dish. Place in the oven and bake, covered, for about 30 minutes or until all the liquid has been absorbed.

✓ MATTAR OR SAAG PANEER (SPINACH CURRY WITH PANEER)

SERVES 6–8

Paneer is fresh cheese, eaten widely in India as a protein source. It has a lovely delicate flavour, rather like cottage cheese, and is easy to make. Like tofu, it acts like a sponge and absorbs the essence of spices.

56

4 cups (1 L) half-and-half cream

FOR THE PANEER:

3 tbsp (45 ml) lemon juice , divided

FOR THE CURRY:

3 tbsp (45 ml) ghee
1 cinnamon stick
seeds from 1 cardamom pod, crushed
2 cloves, ground
1 leek, sliced
1 tsp (5 ml) freshly grated ginger
1 tsp (5 ml) crushed garlic (optional)
2 tsp (10 ml) ground coriander
½ tsp (2.5 ml) red chilli powder, or to taste

½ tsp (2.5 ml) turmeric powder
½ tsp (2.5 ml) ground cumin
2 tbsp (30 ml) ground cashews
1 cup (250 ml) paneer, cubed
2 tomatoes, chopped
sea salt, to taste
1 cup (250 ml) chopped spinach
1 tbsp (15 ml) whipping cream
2 tbsp (30 ml) finely chopped cilantro

FOR THE PANEER:

Allow the cream to come to a boil. Add 2 tbsp (30 ml) lemon juice. Stir continuously until the milk curdles and begins to thicken. Add more lemon juice if mixture doesn't curdle right away. Simmer for an hour or so.

Strain the curdled milk through a fine wire mesh sieve. Put the milk solids or curds in a bowl, cover with another bowl and a heavy weight to press flat to about ½-inch (1 cm) thick—this will take a couple of hours. Once set, you can cut the paneer into cubes. Use immediately, as it will only keep overnight refrigerated.

FOR THE CURRY:

Heat the ghee and add the cinnamon, cardamom seeds and cloves. After 30 seconds or so, add the leeks, ginger, garlic, and cook further until the leek slices are translucent and lightly browned. Add the rest of the spices and ground cashews. Fry for another minute or so, then add the cubed paneer. Add the tomatoes and salt, turn up the heat and fry until mixture thickens. Add the chopped spinach and bring to a boil. Finally, add the cream, mix well, and serve garnished with the chopped cilantro.

This recipe is great with Whole-Wheat Naan (page 36). If you're out of spinach, substitute with peas instead.

SHUBBIE'S EGGS JAMAL

SERVES 6

It was our friend Shubbie who lauded some of the meals we served him as Five Diamond quality. Here is Shubbie's wonderful egg recipe named for another friend, Jamal, who introduced it to him.

1 tbsp (15 ml) butter
2 tbsp (30 ml) olive oil
3 large ripe tomatoes, sliced into
1/4 inch (6 mm) rounds

several leaves fresh basil
6 eggs (the freshest free range you can find)
sea salt and pepper, to taste

Preheat oven to broil.

Brown the butter and olive oil in a large, oven-proof fry pan. Line the pan with the tomato rounds. Cover these with the basil leaves. Cook covered, without stirring or flipping the tomatoes, until they are cooked through and starting to crisp at the edges. The basil will wilt. Crack a whole egg over each tomato slice. Continue to cook uncovered, until eggs fry right on top of the tomatoes. Finish very briefly under the broiler to ensure that the tops of the eggs are cooked—not too runny, but not hard either. Add salt and pepper to taste.

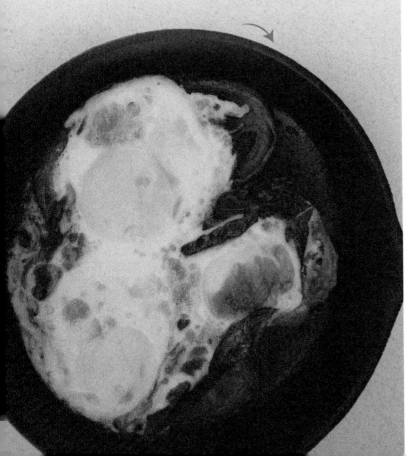

SARASWATI'S CHEESY EGG TORTILLA WRAPS

Serves 4

If we were lucky, our dear friend Saraswati, or Sara for short, made us cheesy scrambled eggs for breakfast when she came to Diamond Forest. We added a little jalapeño and a tortilla and turned it into dinner.

Eggs from properly treated and raised chickens contain just about every nutrient known and are astonishingly nutritious. High quality protein and fat-soluble vitamins A and D abound in the humble egg. Integrity of cell membranes and a sharp brain are also attributed to this wonder food.

4 corn tortillas, buttered lightly on both sides
2 tbsp (30 ml) butter
5 eggs, beaten well
1 tbsp (15 ml) water

1 cup (250 ml) shredded cheese (your choice)
1 tbsp (15 ml) finely chopped,
pickled jalapeño peppers

Wrap the buttered corn tortillas in tinfoil and warm in a toaster oven on toaster setting for about 5–7 minutes.

Heat the butter in a fry pan until browned. Whisk together eggs, water, cheese, and jalapenos. Add to pan and swirl around until cooked through—don't overcook!

Fill each tortilla with the egg mixture, roll up and serve immediately.

SHRI DEVI VEGETABLE LASAGNA

Shri Devi means glorious angel in Sanskrit and is a nickname we use for one of our amazing caretakers who provided this rich and satisfying pasta dish—great for grounding yogis and yoginis who might have done too much pranayama! This can happen, due to the increase of heat and air in the body. One of the benefits of pranayama practice is that it effectively decreases phlegm conditions (too much fluid) but it can also go the other way and produce too much heat and airiness. Heavy foods such as pastas and creamy dishes have an important place in deep retreat as they can reverse the symptoms of this condition, which include nervous tension, irritability, tightness in the chest and head, insomnia, indigestion, and constipation.

60

For the sauce:

3 tbsp (45 ml) olive oil
2 cups (500 ml) roughly chopped mushrooms
3 stalks celery, sliced
1 leek, sliced

6 tomatoes, chopped
2 cups (500 ml) Uncle Harvey's Tomato
Sauce (page 69) or your choice of sauce
1 tsp (5 ml) thyme

For the lasagna:

12 organic brown rice lasagna noodles
6 eggs, boiled and sliced
3 cups (750 ml) Gouda, Monterey Jack
or Asiago (a combination is best)
2 cups (500 ml) chopped fresh spinach

2 cups (500 ml) sliced chard
1 cup (250 ml) grated carrot
1 cup (250 ml) sliced zucchini
¼ cup (60 ml) fresh oregano
¼ cup (60 ml) fresh basil

For the sauce:

Heat the olive oil in a fry pan. Add the mushrooms and sauté until soft and lightly browned on both sides. Add the celery and leeks, continue sautéing until celery is translucent. Add the tomatoes, tomato sauce and thyme. Cover and simmer for about 30 minutes.

For the lasagna:

Preheat oven to 350°F (180°C).

Prepare noodles according to package instructions.

To assemble the layers of the lasagna, select a 9- x 13-inch (23 x 33 cm) casserole dish and begin by covering the bottom of the pan with just enough sauce to cover. Put a layer of 4 noodles on top, slightly overlapping the edges. Add 3 sliced boiled eggs, 1 cup (250 ml) of cheese, and half each of the spinach, chard, carrots, and zucchini. Cover with additional tomato sauce, oregano, and basil. Top with another layer of 4 noodles. Repeat the first layer and top with the last 3 noodles. Add the remaining 1 cup (250 ml) of cheese, and the remaining sauce—at least 1 cup (250 ml). Prepare a tinfoil hood brushed with a little olive oil to prevent sticking and bake for 45 minutes. Remove the tinfoil and bake an additional 10 minutes. Allow to stand for 10 minutes before serving.

CHAPTER 5

THE PERFECTION OF CONCENTRATION: SAUCES, PESTOS, DRESSINGS, SPICES

Suppose you attempt every kind of practice
Where you repeat [mantras] or
do other asceticisms,
Over a long period of time.
If you allow your mind to be distracted
To other subjects, then understanding
The true nature is meaningless.

Once you've developed your practice of effort...
Then place your mind in single-pointedness

A person whose mind is in a state
Of constantly wandering lives his life
In the jaws of mental affliction.
This constant wandering never occurs
With those who remain in isolation
Of body and mind.

My mind is a wild elephant:
I must tie it properly to the strong stake
Of a spiritual object of focus.
I must try with my every effort
To watch that it stays this way,
Without ever getting loose.

No matter what I will make efforts
In single-pointed concentration.
That never for even a second slips.
I will examine my thoughts
Constantly in a certain way, saying
"What is my mind engaged in?"

Master Shantideva, *Guide to the Bodhisattva's Way of Life*

Contemplation:
1. Imagine your body is totally emptied of its contents, filled with only clear blue sky.
2. At the point between your eyebrows is a small, brilliant diamond light.
3. Feel this light as a vortex of energy that allows you indestructible, single pointed concentration and mindfulness as you prepare meals, or any task.
4. You now have the ability to imbue the meals you cook with concentrated love.
5. Now see that ability to focus rippling out to all beings everywhere.

THIS PERFECTION INVOLVES LEARNING TO perfect our ability to concentrate single pointedly on the object of our choice for as long as we like. The *Abhidharma Kosha* (*The Treasure House of Higher Knowledge*) by Master Vasubandhu, circa 350 AD, tells us that concentration is one of the four things that we human beings require to nourish our bodies, along with food, caring for the body, and getting proper rest.

Learning to focus the mind is the first step to concentration. We all know how to do this. As our teacher Geshe Michael often points out, everyone knows how to zero in single-pointedly for hours on "How could they have done that to me? After all I did for them. Do you know what they said? And then they...". You get the picture.

Deep retreat affords a particularly rich opportunity for practicing this form of concentration! It might have been the entire first year of our deep retreat that we ruminated mostly on themes like these. Eventually, it dawned on us that we might be able to use that laser-like beam of focus on something more meaningful and useful. Master Shantideva suggests the Six Perfections for just such a project.

It's not that deep or even long retreat, or any retreat, per se, brings your mind to a single point of concentration—a crucial platform for understanding the higher realities than can free us from suffering states of body and mind. We had a glimpse of this truth when we moved from Vancouver to Gabriola Island about 10 years ago so that we could

concentrate, have peace and silence. No sooner did we move than our neighbours decided to build on their vacant lot next door! It was magnificent. We got an express teaching that the causes of peace and silence in the mind, which are conducive to concentration and meditation, do not intrinsically appear when you move out of the city!

Peace, silence, and concentration come from our minds. Have we seen to it that others have undisturbed peace, that we don't cause ripples in their minds? If we have, then the apparent outward manifestations of a retreat cabin, like ours at Diamond Forest, will appear to be conducive for deep concentration and higher states of meditation. But if we really perfect concentration and meditation, then we will experience it in our minds regardless of the outer world. Our teacher exemplifies this. He often appears to be in an indestructible state of deep concentration and seems able to do such impossible things as translating sacred scriptures from their original languages of Sanskrit and Tibetan into the most poetic and transcendental English (like all the quotations from Master Shantideva in this book) in the middle of Chicago O'Hare International Airport.

That's the kind of laser-like focus that's necessary for deep states of meditation. It only comes from working the first four perfections, watching our mind, and constantly staying alert for our mistaken way of thinking that all the money, the illness, the joy and misery, all the irritation, and all the devastation is originating from somewhere outside of us.

Deepest peace comes when we finally start to put to rest these mistaken beliefs, and that's when we start to perfect concentration and meditation.

This section is devoted to those severely underrated sauces, spices, and dressings that can make a simple dish completely divine. Underrated because, like the practice of cultivating meditative concentration, most of us claim not to have enough time for them! Many of them will keep well for weeks, or even months in deep-freeze, and they are well worth the time it takes to make them as there are no comparable commercial concoctions. They are highly concentrated, so use sparingly and to taste. A little concentration goes a long, long way both in your mouth and in your mind!

What you might notice is missing from most of them, though, are garlic and onions, which we rarely used. In deep retreat, and if we were meditating deeply, these wreaked havoc with our concentrative abilities. Instead, we often used green onions and leeks, which weren't quite as strong and objectionable to our systems.

CURRY POWDER

I always thought I'd like to work in an Indian restaurant so I could learn how to make the lovely spice combinations and masalas that characterize curries. They are all subtly different. This curry powder is fairly mild. If you like it hotter, just increase the number of chillies you use. It's adapted from a recipe I found in an amazing cookbook Roger's sister Suzz and her husband Fuzz, as we like to call them, gave us—*Terrific Pacific Cookbook*.

½ cup (125 ml) coriander seeds
¼ cup (60 ml) cumin seeds
3 tbsp (45 ml) yellow mustard seeds
4 tsp (20 ml) fennel seeds
2 tsp (10 ml) fenugreek seeds

two 2-inch (5 cm) sticks of cinnamon crushed with a mortar and pestle, or
2 tsp (10 ml) ground cinnamon
2 tsp (10 ml) black peppercorns
4 or 5 dried red chillies, to taste
5 tbsp (75 ml) ground turmeric

Heat a small skillet over medium-low heat, add all the ingredients except the turmeric and dry-roast, stirring constantly, until fragrant and several shades darker, about 3 minutes. Add the turmeric, remove from heat and let cool to room temperature. In small batches, grind the mixture in a coffee or spice grinder until fine, about 1 minute.

Store in a tightly covered jar in a cool, dry place or in the freezer. It will keep for about a month without losing its fragrance. We add freshly grated ginger when we use it, rather than adding powdered ginger to the mix.

66

GARAM MASALA

Makes about ½ cup (125 ml)

Generally, it seems to us that garam masala is used to flavour creamier curries and sauces. It has a slightly sweeter flavour than the curry powders and doesn't usually contain chillies. It is added to curries and other dishes towards the very end of the cooking process just before serving.

2 tbsp (30 ml) coriander seeds
2 tbsp (30 ml) cumin seeds
1½ tbsp (22.5 ml) black peppercorns
1½ tbsp (22.5 ml) cardamom seeds

1 tbsp (15 ml) whole cloves
one 2-inch (5 cm) cinnamon stick, crushed into pieces with a mortar and pestle
¼ tsp (1 ml) nutmeg, freshly grated

Heat a small skillet over medium-low heat, add all the spices except the nutmeg and dry-roast, stirring constantly, until fragrant and several shades darker, about 2 minutes. Add the nutmeg, remove from heat, and let cool to room temperature. Grind the spices in a coffee or spice grinder until fine, about 1 minute.

Store in a tightly covered jar in a cool, dry place or freezer. The mixture will keep for about a month without losing its fragrance.

TRIDOSHIC SPICE BLEND

Makes about ½ cup (125 ml)

This is a general recipe that can be adjusted to suit any dosha (your particular unique metabolic type) or palette. You can learn how to adapt recipes to your dosha by consulting an Ayurvedic practitioner.

For the most flavourful and active results, try to look for organic, fair-trade, and biodynamic sourced spices. Keep this spice blend on hand and add a teaspoon to grains or greens when you're cooking. Unlike store bought curry powder mixes, this tridoshic spice blend has a pleasantly mild taste and is full of anti-inflammatory agents.

2 1/2 tbsp (45 ml) turmeric
11/2 tbsp (22.5 ml) cumin
11/2 tbsp (22.5 ml) coriander
1 tsp (5 ml) fennel
1 tsp (5 ml) powdered mustard
1 tsp (5 ml) powdered ginger

1 tsp (5 ml) cinnamon
1/2 tsp (2.5 ml) ground fenugreek
Optional: 1/2 tsp (2.5 ml) ground cardamom
Optional: A pinch each of ground nutmeg, ground clove, cayenne

Combine all ingredients and store in a glass jar.

UNCLE HARVEY'S TOMATO SAUCE

Makes about 1 cup (250 ml)

I learned how to make this sauce from my Bodhisattva Uncle Harvey, who just happened to have lived in Tucson, Arizona for 50 years when we suddenly showed up in 2005. We started going three times a year for around seven weeks at a time to study with our teachers and this sauce was a staple of our mealtimes.

We made this sauce in huge batches starting in the late summer when our (many) tomato plants started ripening by the hundreds in our Diamond Forest greenhouses. We stored it in small re-sealable plastic bags in our deep freezer, so we had some handy year-round, to use, and give away. Nothing compares to a homegrown, organic sun-ripened tomato, and they are bursting happily with many vitamins and minerals.

I don't recommend using aluminum cookware for any cooking, but especially in this recipe where the acidic tomatoes can react with the metal and leach aluminum oxides into the food, and then into us.

12 ripe tomatoes   sea salt and pepper, to taste
1/2 cup (125 ml) organic butter   basil, fresh or dried or other herbs

Use as many ripe tomatoes as you have available. Drop them, one by one, into rapidly boiling water for a minute or two. As soon as their skins start to peel off, drop them into a large bowl or sink full of ice water. The skins will practically slip off by themselves.

Brown the butter in a large pot, and drop the whole skinned tomatoes into the butter. Lower heat and simmer the tomatoes until they have reduced quite a bit—this may take an hour or more. Add salt and pepper to taste, and chopped basil or other fresh or dried herbs if you like.

Uncle Harvey served this sauce straight up on pasta. I like to add in whatever is on hand—finely sliced celery, mushrooms, peppers, zucchini, and all kinds of herbs!

BIG RED MOTHER SAUCE

MAKES 3 CUPS (750 ML)

This sauce was inspired by a recipe from *Rebar: Modern Food Cookbook*. My dear friend and former client Nancy Chan gave it to me before she withdrew her current emanation. We used it in deep retreat constantly. I've never been to the Rebar restaurant in Victoria, British Columbia but Nancy used to rave about it, and I hope to one day go there for dinner and tell those extraordinary Rebar ladies what I think of them and their recipes! This sauce is especially delicious on enchiladas, burritos, quesadillas, as a base for a dal or baked beans—you name it!

2 tbsp (30 ml) butter
4 green onions, chopped
¼ cup (60 ml) masa harina (Mexican corn flour)
1 tbsp (15 ml) olive oil
2–3 tbsp (30–45 ml) Mexican chilli powder, to taste
1 tsp (5 ml) sea salt
½ tsp (2.5 ml) ground cumin
¼ tsp (1 ml) cayenne pepper
1 tbsp (15 ml) minced fresh oregano or
½ tbsp (7.5 ml) dried oregano
4 cups (1 L) vegetable stock, hot
2 tbsp (30 ml) canned tomato paste or
Uncle Harvey's Tomato Sauce (page 69)
1 tsp (5 ml) rapadura or coconut sugar (optional)

Brown butter in a saucepan and sauté green onions until soft and lightly browned. Sprinkle in the masa harina, add olive oil and sugar if desired, and stir continuously until it turns golden. Add the spices, oregano, and continue stirring. Add the hot vegetable stock, tomato paste, and bring to a boil. Reduce heat and simmer partially covered for half an hour or so, stirring regularly.

JAPANESE CARROT AND GINGER DRESSING

If you don't have a blender or food processor, grate the carrots and daikon in a superfine ginger grater and make this dressing in smaller batches.

1 cup (250 ml) peeled and cubed carrots
¾ cup (185 ml) olive oil
½ cup (125 ml) peeled and cubed Japanese daikon radish
¼ cup (60 ml) seasoned Japanese vinegar
2 tbsp (30 ml) freshly grated ginger
2 tbsp (30 ml) toasted sesame oil
1 tbsp (15 ml) apple cider vinegar
1 tsp (5 ml) soy sauce
1 green onion, chopped
1 small clove garlic (optional)
¼ tsp (1 ml) powdered hot mustard
sea salt and pepper, to taste

Process everything in a food processor or blender until the consistency is smooth and thick.

GINGERY MISO DRESSING

MAKES 1 1/2 CUPS (375 ML)

Miso is amazingly versatile. Its fermenting process assists in the assimilation and digestion of tofu, and that's probably why it often appears with it. Tasty on tofu salads.

½ cup (125 ml) extra-virgin olive oil
¼ cup (60 ml) balsamic vinegar
2 tbsp (30 ml) miso
1 leek

1 tbsp (15 ml) freshly grated ginger
1 tsp (5 ml) tahini
½ cup (125 ml) water

Blend or process all ingredients until smooth, adding water as needed.

YOGURT-CILANTRO CHUTNEY

MAKES 1 CUP (250 ML)

I first created this recipe for my mother when she came for a visit during our retreat. We served her curry with this HOT chutney, without the yogurt. We had to add yogurt liberally so we could eat the rest of the chutney!

½ cup (125 ml) fresh cilantro
¼ cup (60 ml) rich yogurt
1 tbsp (15 ml) freshly squeezed lemon or lime juice

1 tsp (5 ml) fresh hot chilli or ½ tsp
(2.5 ml) red pepper flakes
1 green onion, roughly chopped
1–3 tbsp (15–45 ml) olive oil

Combine all ingredients, except the olive oil, in a food processor and process to a coarse pesto consistency. Add olive oil 1 tbsp (15 ml) at a time for desired consistency.

73

PEANUT DIPPING SAUCE

MAKES 1 CUP (250 ML)

There are so many ways to enjoy the nutritious benefits and delicious flavour of nuts, which are highin essential fatty acids and vitamin F. Try substituting other nuts in this recipe for variety.

½ cup (125 ml) peanuts   1 tbsp (15 ml) toasted sesame oil

1 tbsp (15 ml) soy sauce or tamari   1 tbsp (15 ml) rice vinegar

Combine all ingredients in a food processor or blender until you get a chunky sauce.

 This sauce is great for pesto tortilla wraps or for dipping fresh raw or lightly steamed vegetables.

AVOCADO-CILANTRO CREAM

MAKES 1 CUP (250 ML)

The word sublime was created for this recipe. Try it as a dip for burritos or naan.

½ cup (125 ml) sour cream
1 ripe avocado, pitted and flesh scooped out
3 tbsp (45 ml) whipping cream
3 tbsp (45 ml) cilantro
3 tbsp (45 ml) fresh lime juice
1 small clove garlic (optional)
sea salt and pepper, to taste

Combine all ingredients in a food processor and process until mixture is perfectly smooth.

CHAPTER 6

The Perfection of Wisdom: Cakes, Cookies, and Other Sweet Treats

Suppose any particular person fails
To understand this secret of the mind;
The highest import, the principal teaching.

They may hope to reach bliss
and smash all suffering,
But they will wander nonetheless, just as they
Always have, without reaching their goal.

When is it then I'll be able
To put an end to suffering
With a rain of goodness,
Of all that's kept me well,
From clouds of my good deeds to those
Who are caught in the fire of suffering?

Master Shantideva, *Guide to the
Bodhisattva's Way of Life*

Contemplation:
1. Imagine someone you know who is dangerously obese. Experience empathy—a wish that you could help them, educate them in some way.
2. Make a resolution to do exactly that. Invite them to go for a leisurely stroll or suggest going grocery shopping together.
3. Recognize the source of all we see. We wouldn't see obese, suffering people in our world if we ourselves had never exhibited our own addictive behaviours.
4. Feel the deep relief of this realization, this great secret, the principal teaching—that there is something we can do about the suffering we see and experience.

TO PERFECT WISDOM IS TO FINALLY perfect all the perfections. What does it mean to perfect the Perfections?

Merely feeding the hungry, keeping high standards of morality, controlling our angry outbursts, or enjoying our chosen line of work, and even perfecting our meditative concentration will not bring us to the perfection of wisdom. In fact, paradoxically, the perfection of the first five requires the perfection of the last one.

The sweet treat of bliss and wisdom—which in its highest expression is full enlightenment—is the highest goal. It comes through determination, through adhering to a perfect recipe, without deviation. Following the instructions. This was hard for us! We're not very good at sticking to the recipe, in cooking or otherwise.

Eventually in our evolution as humans we develop a craving for the sweetest treat of all—a direct understanding of why we and others are alive at all, or at least why we are in deep retreat! We constantly asked ourselves this question: what are we doing here?

The Six Perfections provide the ingredients and the method. The ingredients start with finding someone who can teach us, someone we see as having perfected the Perfections who can help us.

> The mental afflictions are such that
> Once I have eliminated them,
> Cleared them from my mind
> By using the eye of wisdom,
> They have nowhere else to go—
> No place they can make their home,
> No way to return and harm me.

> It all comes down to the fact
> That my mind is so very weak:
> I do not have the energy.

Master Shantideva, *Guide to the Bodhisattva's Way of Life*

And so, we respectfully ask our Teachers for their help and offer them what we can as a token of our gratitude. We rely on their instructions, their recipes, and we actually start following their directions.

> Moreover what better method could there
> Be to repay the kindness of those
> Who act unimpelled as closest friends
> And help to an infinite degree,
> Than to please all living beings?

Master Shantideva, *Guide to the Bodhisattva's Way of Life*

And then we begin. Step by step, we progress through the recipes. Perfecting the perfections, perfecting ourselves, and perfecting our world. As one of our teachers always says, "You're not perfect until I am".

> In this way we must engage in different
> Kinds of contemplations and make great efforts
> For the purpose of accomplishing the rules [following the recipe]
> As they have been described.
> If you—a patient who absolutely had
> To be treated with specific kinds of medicine—
> Refused to listen to your physician's advice
> How could you ever be cured?

They are the single medicine
For the pains of living kind,
And the source of every happiness;
So may the teachings remain
Far into the future,
With prosperity and glory.

Master Shantideva, *Guide to the Bodhisattva's Way of Life*

Especially while in retreat, perfecting wisdom in sweet-treat creations starts, first of all, with the omission or substitution of refined, white sugar. The only exceptions to this rule are for the recipes containing chocolate, which require a high degree of wisdom to enjoy judiciously! We substitute refined sugar with natural sweeteners—maple syrup, raw honey, coconut sugar, date sugar, molasses, rapadura, mashed dates, bananas, freshly made apple sauce, raisins, stewed prunes, and prune juice, 100% pear nectar or other fruit juices, and even sweet potato. Even so, a very little sugar from any source goes an extremely long way, and I recommend limiting your intake of any sugars, especially concentrated sugars like desserts.

It is exceedingly wise to replace white flour, even the unbleached variety, with other freshly ground whole grains. I used mostly stone-ground organic whole wheat, buckwheat, and rye flours, always pre-soaked for 12–24 hours in yogurt, whey, or buttermilk. You can substitute lemon juice in water if you are allergic to dairy products or are a vegan. The exception to this rule is the organic unbleached white flour used in the pie crust recipe

and very rarely, I use a 50-50 or 25-35 split of white and whole-wheat flours.

I adapted recipes to use organic butter (preferably from pasture-fed cows) or organic coconut oil instead of lard or other oils.

I used totally fresh whole eggs (never powdered!) laid a day or two earlier by lovingly cared for hens from a neighbouring farm. These chickens are allowed to roam freely and partake in all the special chicken foods in the forest that they were intended to eat, rather than commercial grains. Try to source organic free-run eggs.

I used organic milk and cream products, only because we weren't able to acquire a cow and start milking!

I used baking soda (page XXIV) or natural leaveners like eggs instead of baking powder wherever possible, and we use raw, unrefined sea salt.

I soaked most of the grains, flours, and oats for 12–24 hours before use, as well as all nuts and seeds. I've learned the wisdom of most of these practices from many different teachers over the last few decades including Paul Chek, Sally Fallon, Dr. Weston Price, the Ayurvedic tradition, and the cooking and food preparation wisdom of our mothers and ancestors.

Finally, it is a wise practice to limit any foods rich in sugars, natural or otherwise, to festive occasions. This keeps them special!

AVOCADO ICE CREAM

SERVES 2–4

This is the simplest, most sumptuous dessert you will ever make. It's simply unbelievable and doubly delicious when you've been in deep retreat for three years and only had ice cream once!

2 large ripe avocados, pitted
and flesh scooped out
¼ cup (60 ml) raw honey
3 tbsp (45 ml) lime juice, freshly squeezed

1 tsp (5 ml) grated lime rind
pinch sea salt
¼ cup (60 ml) walnuts (optional)

Process all ingredients except walnuts in a food processor until perfectly smooth.

Add the walnuts if desired and process just long enough to coarsely chop the walnuts. Freeze in an airtight plastic container for about 4 hours.

FRILARY BLISS BALLS ↘

MAKES 12–20 BALLS

Just before we went into our deep retreat in December 2010, our special friends Hilary and Fred (affectionately known as Frilary) gave us a batch of these delicious balls of bliss, and continued to send in batches throughout our retreat, ensuring our ongoing bliss, and therefore their own! I tampered with their original recipe a tiny bit (okay, maybe a lot!) to make it vegan friendly as well.

½ cup (125 ml) raw almonds, soaked overnight in salted water, then rinsed well and drained
½ cup (125 ml) raisins
½ cup (125 ml) almond milk
¼ cup (125 ml) raw honey
1/3 cup (80 ml) melted butter
1/3 cup (80 ml) tahini

2 tsp (10 ml) ground cinnamon
1 tsp (5 ml) ground cardamom
1 tsp (5 ml) vanilla
2 cups (500 ml) quick oats
1½ cups (375 ml) grated unsweetened coconut, divided
½ cup (125 ml) chocolate chips (optional)

Finely grind the almonds in a food processor. Add the raisins and process further. Add the almond milk, honey, butter, tahini, cinnamon, cardamom, and vanilla. Pulse until everything is blended and well mixed. Add the oats and 1 cup (250 ml) of the coconut for a few pulses until it's all blended.

Transfer to a bowl and add the chocolate chips, mixing gently. Taste and adjust sweetness to taste.

Chill for several hours. Lay out the remaining ½ cup (125 ml) of grated coconut on a baking tray. Form balls from the chilled dough and roll the balls in the coconut "like a kid playing in mud," say Frilary. Freeze or refrigerate.

APRICOT ALMOND SQUARES

SERVES 10–12

Hugely popular, people usually begged me not to tempt them anymore with these. I took that as a compliment. I cut them into one or two-inch squares to relish, rather than the customary huge slabs. Otherwise, we wouldn't have been able to eat another single thing for at least 24 hours!

1 cup (250 ml) butter, melted
¼ cup (60 ml) yogurt
2 cups (500 ml) rolled or quick oats
1½ cups (375 ml) whole-wheat flour
2 cups (500 ml) almonds, pre-soaked and toasted
2 tsp (10 ml) baking soda
1½ tsp (7.5 ml) ground cinnamon

2 tbsp (30 ml) softened butter
1 cup (250 ml) coconut sugar
1 egg, lightly beaten
1 cup (250 ml) apricot jam or 1 cup (250 ml) dried apricots cooked until tender and then processed in a food processor with a dribble of maple syrup.

In a medium-sized bowl, mix together the butter and yogurt. Add the oats and flour and mix until just blended. Cover this mixture with a towel and leave at room temperature for 12 hours.

Preheat oven to 350°F (180°C). Grind the almonds in a food processor. Add the flour mixture, baking soda, cinnamon, softened butter, coconut sugar, and process further. Split the dough in half, setting one half aside—this will be the crumbly topping.

Add the beaten egg to the second half of the dough and process in a food processor until pea sized dough balls form. Press into the bottom of a buttered 9- x 13-inch (23 x 33 cm) baking dish. Bake for 10 minutes until golden.

Spread the apricot jam evenly over the surface of the baked crust and sprinkle with the remaining crumbly mixture. Bake another 10 minutes until golden brown. Chill or freeze before cutting into 1- or 2-inch (2.5 or 5 cm) squares.

Tried, tested, and approved by Shyam, one of our classmates, who ate an entire bowl that we had made and reserved for our teachers! His verdict? "That was unbelievable". Versions of this rice pudding have also been endorsed by Mama Hilde, who didn't even like rice pudding until she tried this one!

Coconut is rich in chloride, essential for proper growth and brain function. It helps regulate acid/alkaline balance in the blood and is involved in the digestion of protein.

½ cup (125 ml) organic uncooked brown rice, coarsely ground a little at a time in a coffee or spice grinder

½ cup (125 ml) raisins soaked, dried and chopped

½ cup (125 ml) fine-ground almonds

¼ cup (60 ml) freshly grated coconut (optional)

1-inch (2.5 cm) whole ginger root peeled and crushed with the flat side of a knife

1 cinnamon stick

1 vanilla bean (optional)

3 whole black peppercorns

2 whole cloves, ground

½ tsp (2.5 ml) ground cardamom

½ tsp (2.5 ml) ground nutmeg

1 cup (250 ml) milk

one 12 oz (355 ml) can full-fat organic coconut milk

½ cup (125 ml) coconut sugar, to taste

2 tbsp (30 ml) rose water or orange blossom water

Soak ground rice in 2 cups (500 ml) of water, covered with a towel, in a warm place for 7 hours or overnight.

Transfer this mixture to a stainless steel saucepan and add the raisins, ground almonds, grated coconut, ginger root, cinnamon stick, vanilla bean, peppercorns, cloves, cardamom, and nutmeg. Bring to boil, reduce heat to low and cook covered for 30 minutes.

Add the milk and coconut milk and bring to a boil again, stirring constantly with a wooden spatula. Scrape the bottom of the pan continuously to avoid sticking and burning. Reduce heat to a simmer, cook another half hour or so, stirring all the time and monitoring the liquid content. It should not be runny, nor should it be too thick. You may need to add more water or milk.

When the rice is cooked, add the sugar to taste, the rose water, and a little more milk or cream if necessary to bring it to a thick, creamy consistency.

OAT SPICE CAKE WITH CASHEW COCONUT CRUNCH TOPPING

I didn't use the white flour called for in the traditional recipe; instead, I used soaked whole-wheat flour. The incredibly springy lightness of this cake will amaze you!

FOR THE CAKE BATTER:

1 cup (250 ml) yogurt
½ cup (125 ml) boiling water
2 cups (500 ml) rolled or quick oats
½ cup (125 ml) whole-wheat flour
2/3 cup (160 ml) butter, softened

½ cup (125 ml) maple syrup
1 tsp (5 ml) baking soda
1 tsp (5 ml) ground cinnamon
1 tsp (5 ml) allspice
dash sea salt

FOR THE CASHEW AND COCONUT TOPPING:

1 cup (250 ml) crispy cashews, chopped
1 cup (250 ml) shredded coconut, toasted
½ cup (125 ml) coconut sugar
½ cup (125 ml) whipping cream

1/3 cup (80 ml) butter
Soak the cashews for 5–6 hours in
salted water, rinse well, and toast at
170°F (77°C) for about 8 hours.

FOR THE CAKE BATTER:

In a medium-sized bowl, mix the yogurt with the boiling water. Add the oats and the whole-wheat flour, cover with a towel and leave for 24 hours in a warm place.

Preheat oven to 350°F (180°C) and butter a 9-inch (23 cm) springform pan. Add the butter, maple syrup, baking soda, and spices to the oat and flour mixture. Fold together gently and pour the batter into the prepared baking pan.

Bake for about 30–40 minutes or until a toothpick inserted in the centre comes out clean. Remove the cake from the oven and set the oven to broil.

FOR THE CASHEW AND COCONUT TOPPING:

Combine all the ingredients for the topping in a saucepan and heat until butter melts and everything is well blended. Pour the mixture over the baked cake when it comes out of the oven. Place the cake beneath the broiler, watching it the whole time, until the topping turns golden brown. This will only take about 2 minutes and will caramelize quickly, so keep watching! Cool cake before serving with a little whipped cream.

 This recipe can also be baked in a muffin tin or a loaf pan.

WILD BLACKBERRY AND ORCHARD APPLE PIE

As a counter-pose to many hours of intensive meditative practices, we decompressed by going on long walks in an isolated and remote 707-acre natural park behind our retreat house. In the late summer and early fall, these walks turned into wild blackberry picking expeditions in the forests surrounding the retreat centre here on Gabriola Island. We froze the blackberries in resealable plastic bags so we could enjoy them through the winter for pies, or as a coulis on cheesecake, pancakes, or porridge. We also often put in salal berries. Salal grows wild all over British Columbia and their berries grace the salal bushes in August. These give a thick, juicy, sweet, musky flavour.

We owe gratitude to all berries for their wealth of minerals, vitamin C and carotenoids. Wild or organically grown berries also give us nitrilosides—a B-complex vitamin that fights cancer—as well asellagic acid, an anti-oxidant that detoxifies carcinogens. Add to this wealth of nourishment and protection a life spent in caring for the needs of others and ensuring they have all they need to stay healthy and you're destined for deathlessness.

For the pie crust:

1 1/3 cups (330 ml) unbleached white flour
pinch sea salt
½ cup (125 ml) frozen butter

2 egg yolks, beaten
3 tbsp (45 ml) ice water

For the pie filling:

2 lb (1 kg) wild blackberries or any fresh berries
2 cups (500 ml) thinly sliced apples
¼ cup (60 ml) coconut sugar
¼ cup (60 ml) arrowroot powder or cornstarch

1 tbsp (15 ml) freshly squeezed lemon juice
zest of 1 medium orange
juice of 1 medium orange

FOR THE PIE CRUST:

Sift the flour and salt into a food processor. Give it a few pulses to combine. Cut the butter into about 16 little cubes and distribute it over the flour. Pulse a few times, only until the butter is in pea-sized pieces and well distributed. Dribble the beaten egg yolks over the flour mixture and pulse a few times. Turn on the food processor and pour the ice water in, then immediately stop the processor. You should still be able to see the butter as pea-sized pieces.

Place the dough onto a piece of wax paper, wrap it up and squeeze it to form a ball. Refrigerate for 2–3 hours.

Preheat oven to 350°F (180°C). Roll the dough out on a floured surface using flour to keep it from sticking. Line it into 1 large or 2 smaller pie pans and chill in the refrigerator.

FOR THE PIE FILLING:

Toss all filling ingredients well to mix thoroughly, making sure there are no clumps of thickener. Smooth the filling into a chilled, unbaked pie crust shell. Bake for 25–45 minutes depending on the size of your pie pans, making sure the bottom of the crust is browned.

This is the only recipe in this book that calls for more than a few tablespoons of unbleached white flour!

APPLE-DATE PUDDING CAKE

SERVES 8–10

This cake developed from having four different cookbooks open at once! It is extraordinarily mouth-watering, moist, and delicious. It's so moist I couldn't even decide whether to call it pudding or cake!

Apples are rich in boron, which helps prevent osteoporosis. They are one of the top 10 most contaminated foods from pesticides and toxic residues, though, so please serve and eat organic apples! Although most fruits and vegetables contain very few enzymes, many tropical fruits such as dates, kiwis, bananas, avocados, papaya, and pineapple are exceptions. Enzyme rich foods give lots energy!

1/3 cup (80 ml) pitted dates
1/4 cup (60 ml) boiling water
1½ cups (375 ml) whole-wheat flour
1½ cups (375 ml) yogurt
2 cups (500 ml) grated apples
2/3 cup (160 ml) coconut sugar
2 tsp (10 ml) grated orange rind
1 tsp (5 ml) baking soda

1 tsp (5 ml) ground cinnamon
1 tsp (5 ml) ground cardamom
½ tsp (2.5 ml) freshly grated ginger
½ tsp (2.5 ml) sea salt
2 tbsp (30 ml) butter, melted
1 tbsp (15 ml) arrowroot powder or 1 tbsp (15 ml) cornstarch dissolved in ¼ cup (60 ml) milk
1 tbsp (15 ml) vanilla extract

Soak the dates in the boiling water and mash. In a small bowl, combine flour and yogurt to soak, covered with a towel, in a warm place for 24 hours.

Preheat oven to 350°F (180°C). Transfer flour-yogurt mixture to a mixer bowl. Add the apples, sugar, orange rind, baking soda, cinnamon, cardamom, ginger, and salt. Mix with electric mixer or hand-held beater until combined. Add the rest of the ingredients and mix again on the lowest speed until well blended. Scrape the batter into a buttered 8-inch (20 cm) round baking pan and bake for 45–60 minutes, or until a toothpick inserted in a few places comes out clean.

CHAPTER 7

The Last Word

We spend our days in gentle walks and thoughts
Of helping others, here in the silent
Peace of the forest, flowing in soft breezes;
We live doing as we please in our mansion
Of a wide flat rock, cool with the touch
Of moonlight and sandalwood scent of the holy,
Living deep within the woods
Of peacefulness, completely emptied
Of conflict and afflictions. [Well,
we're working on it]

We live where we please, as long
As we like, in abandoned houses
Or caves, or else at the foot of a tree.
We have given up the suffering
Of owning and protecting things,
Carefree we live, relying on nothing.

Think of these considerations
And others as well, contemplate
The benefits of isolation.

Put an end to useless
Thoughts, and meditate upon
The wish for enlightenment.

From the very beginning exert yourself
In the practice of treating others
And yourself the same.
When the happiness and the sufferings
Are the same, then you will care for all
Just as you do yourself.

Of giving and the rest
So they are heightened ever further,
And never give up the greater for the less:
Concentrate on others' aims.

Master Shantideva, *Guide to the Bodhisattva's Way of Life*

IT HAPPENS LIKE THIS. THE QUALITIES WE experienced in our deep retreat surroundings and the care we had been blessed with have no inherent nature of being one way or another. In fact, there were times when we experienced hell on earth or extreme claustrophobia and anxiety in this retreat in paradise! The way these things look to us come from seeds we have planted by providing ideal conditions for others—maybe accidentally, maybe intentionally.

Just as we start with the *man in the mirror* to obliterate all hatred in our world, we also create the causes for all our blessings and the divine world we inhabit. There are no accidents or coincidences. As we intentionally work with the affliction in our minds to change the affliction in our world, we become acutely conscious of exactly what and how we wish our world to look. We can then begin to plant the right seeds to grow this garden. In fact, the more skillfully and precisely we do this, the less damage control we have to do! When we rejoice in the wonders of our world and especially rejoice in the amazing accomplishments of others, it creates the causes for more of the same.

In the 10th and last chapter of Master Shantideva's *Guide to the Bodhisattva's Way of Life*, he teaches us a fascinating way of banking our efforts, or you could say reinvesting our profits, or re-sowing the seeds from the harvest. He calls it *dedication*. It's how we end and seal all our practices—meditation, yoga asana, pranayama, and mudra practices, mantra recitation, cooking, baking, gardening.

Remember? We started our practices by setting our motivation the way the guide teaches—the wish. There is no other reason to do any of this other than to perfect our world, and no way to do this other than to perfect ourselves. We end all our practices through the very specific targeted dedication of any goodness we may have gathered by offering it to others. Essentially, we pay it forward.

Whether we've just cooked a lovely meal or baked a delectable sweet treat; whether we've given away a couple of dozen of our precious fresh eggs from our neighbours or grown six extra rows of carrots and forty extra tomatoes for gifts; whether we have maintained a state of mindful serenity while preparing food for others; all these activities, in fact, anything we do, could be harnessed to produce specific results in the future, but only if we think of it that way.

By the power of having completed this little cookbook, I experience this act of truth that through the grace of my teachers, may I—with infinite dances of countless enlightened physical forms—take in and care for all living beings who stretch as far as endless space.

It would be impossible and silly for me to try to put it any better than Master Shantideva does in his 10th chapter, and so, I reprint our teacher Geshe Michael's translation of this gem for you here.

CHAPTER 8

DEDICATING THE POWER OF GOOD DEEDS

Thus have I completed writing
A *Guide to the Bodhisattva's Way of Life*.
And I pray that by this goodness
Every living being
May take up this way of life.

By the power of this good deed too
May any single living creature
In sickness or in pain,
Of body or of mind,
In any corner of this universe,
Be thrown into a sea of bliss.

And for as long as they wander
In the circle of suffering life,
May they never lose this bliss.
May every one of them one day reach
The bliss beyond all other,
And stay there never-ending.

I don't know how many
Realms of hell there are
Hidden in our world;
But by this power may every person
Trapped in one instead find joy
In the joy of the Heaven of Joy.

May those who freeze in the cold of hell
Be covered in warmth.
May infinite showers of gentle rain
Fall from vast Bodhisattva clouds
To cool the searing pain
Of those who live there in fire.

May the forest of falling leaves of knives
Turn for those who live there into
A pleasure grove of shady bowers.
May the daggers of the trunks
Of the trees of Shalmali
Sprout as the Wish-Giving Tree instead.

May the caverns of hell suddenly echo forth
With the soft sweet song of the dove
and nightingale,
Ruby-throated sparrow, graceful swans, birds
Of every kind, drawn to the gentle waters
That spring up instantly there, covered
with lotuses
Whose delicate fragrance fills the air.

May heaps of burning embers of the fire
become piles
Of precious jewels, and the red-hot glowing
iron floor

The ground of a new world, spar-
kling in crystal light.
May the mountains that slam
together, crushing the crowds
Of helpless people between them, turn to the palace
Temples of heaven, filled with bliss-filled Buddhas.

In the moment that I speak may
the great rain of putrid
Filth, and stones of solid fire, knives, and spears,
Transform into a soft steady shower
of fragrant flower petals.
And in the hells of anger, where
people snatch up rocks
And sticks to gash one another
open, may they instead
Gather up armfuls of petals, laugh-
ing, tossing over each other.

I send the awesome power of the
good deed that I've done
As well to all those trapped within
the river that cannot
Be crossed, wrapped within the
hell-flame there, with all
The skin and flesh ripped away
from their bodies, the bones
Jutting out in the glistening white
of freshly fallen snow;
May this power grow their bodies
back, in the form of divine Angels.

And then may the beings in hell take pause,
and wonder suddenly to themselves,
"Why now do the henchmen
of the Lord of Death and his vicious
ravens, and birds of prey,
why do they turn and run from us?
What glorious power has turned the night of hell
to golden day, and smothered us within
This happiness, this strength, this bliss
Who could have such power?" And may they raise
their eyes and see the blue
Of sky, and seated in it
the One Who Holds the Diamond in His Hand.
And then may joy spread
in their hearts, so powerful that
It tears away every wrong they ever did,
and so then they can rise
And fly—fly away with him.

May a rain of lovely flower petals
mixed with cool and perfumed water
Descend in a song and extinguish the flames
of the fires that burn in hell.
May the beings who live there look upon
this sight, and suddenly
Be overcome by happiness. And then
may they think to themselves,
"Who could have done this thing?"
And may they turn and see
Before them the One who holds
the Lotus in His Hand.

And then may the hell beings
hear a voice that calls to them and says:
"Come my friends, so far away,
cast away your fears now,
and come be at my side;
Come to the one whose power
has stripped away your agony
and thrown you into joy."

And when they lay their eyes on this one,
on Gentle Voice himself,
may every miserable creature there
Burst forth in a song, a song
that roars throughout the hells,
a song that sings:
"You are the Bodhisattva who protects
every single living being,
overcome by your love for them;

You are the youth divine,
with your flowing locks,
body blazing in light;
How could it be
that you have come to us,
and smashed terrors here?
Are you not the one
to whom a thousand gods
would run, to touch
The tips of their crowns
at your lotus feet?
The one whose eyes glisten
in tears for compassion for us?

The one on whom
a constant shower of petals falls?
See him now—surrounded by palaces
filled with crowds of celestial maidens
singing out his praises!"

Oh thus may it come to pass,
through the power of the goodness
that I've done.
Every suffering being in hell,
Wrapped now in deep happiness,
standing staring up
At clouds as they gather overhead,
And the reality
Of the Bodhisattvas—
The one whose name is
Sheer Excellence,
And all the rest,

Uncovered fully in the light,
Sending down upon them
Showers of rain
That brings them bliss,
Cool soft rain,
Rain of finest fragrance.

And by this power may every being
Who lives in the animal realm be freed
from the terror of feeding off each other
May those who live as craving spirits
Enjoy a life of peace and plenty.
Like humans of the isle of Haunting Voice.

May a stream of milk descend from the hand
Of the Lord of Power, the Realized One,
The One Who Looks with Loving Eyes,
And may it fill the spirits who crave,
Washing them too in a gentle bath,
Leaving them cool and refreshed.

And by this power may the blind
Open their eyes and see the beauty;
May the deaf hear the song of sound.
May every woman with child give birth
As Maya, the Buddha's angel mother,
Did Him – without a hint of pain.

May those without sufficient clothing
Be suddenly clothed, may the hungry
Be instantly filled with food.
May those who suffer now from thirst
Drink fine fresh water
And other delicious beverages.

May every poor person there is
Find all the money they need;
May those who grieve be comforted.
May those who've lost hope
Find hope anew, and security
That will never leave them.

May every single being who's sick
Within this entire universe
Be suddenly, totally, cured.
May every kind of disease
Ever known to living kind
Vanish now, forever.

May all those in any kind of fear
Be suddenly freed from it.
May those imprisoned be released.
May those downtrodden come to power,
All of us living then as family,
In harmony with each other.

May all of those who are on the road,
To anywhere at all, be safe
And comfortable, wherever they are now.
And may they without the slightest trouble
Find at the end of their journey the thing
They left their home to find.

May all those who've left dry land
To travel in boats or ships
Accomplish all they set out to do.
May they cross the dangers of the waters
And then return safely to their homes
And the arms of friends and family.

May those who travel a barren waste,
Or mistake their way, who wander lost,
Suddenly come upon new companions
And find their way easily, free of fatigue,
Without the slightest danger of things
Like thieves or wild beasts.

May holy angels come and protect
All those who live in fear, with nowhere
To go, no path to follow:
Small children, the elderly, those with no one
To help them; those who cannot sleep,
Those who are troubled, and the insane.

May they spend every life they still have to live
Free of every obstacle to a spiritual life:
May they find firm feelings of faith,
And wisdom, and a perfect capacity
For love; may their physical needs
Be filled, may they lead good lives.

May they have all they need to live, forever,
Without a moment's pause, as if they possessed
The treasure of the magic sky.
May they live together without ever quarreling,
Without ever hurting each other, enjoying instead
The freedom to live as they choose to.

May every person who is small or shy,
Who has no confidence, become
Strong and full of grace.
May those who've lived a life of need
And suffered from it physically
Recover in resplendent health.

May all who live in a place of society
Where they're not treated right transform
Forever to a position ideal.
May those who are looked down upon
Be raised up high, and their arrogant friends
Be tumbled to the ground.

And by this goodness I have done
May every single suffering being
Give up every single harmful
Thought or word or deed;
Taking up always in its stead
Thoughts and words and deeds of virtue.

May these beings never cease to strive
To reach the ultimate goal, for others;
And may their hearts be swept away
By the stream of loving conduct.
May they abandon every sort of dark behaviour,
Remaining in the care of every Holy Being.

May every living soul enjoy
A life immeasurably long,
Living thus forever in
A state of constant bliss,
So that even the very word "death"
Is never heard spoken again.

May all the places that exist, in every world
there is,
Turn instantly into gardens of elegant design,
Filled with trees that grant your every wish.
And may the Enlightened Ones, along with
their daughters
And their sons, walk amidst the trees,
Singing out the sweet song of the Dharma.

In each one of these places
May the very foundation, the earth itself,
Be transformed, from sharp stones and the like,
Into the heavenly ground of lapis lazuli—
As smooth as the palm of your hand,
And soft to walk upon.

And like a precious jewel
Adorning this same ground,
May all the secret worlds that exist
And all the goodness in them
Abide atop these newfound lands,
Crowded with Warrior Angels.

And too, may all who live and breathe
Hear the song of birds,
The wind in the trees,
The light of the sun, and the sky itself,
Singing aloud to them an endless
Rhapsody of holy teachings.

And wherever they go may they always meet
The Enlightened Ones, and their children
Who strive for enlightenment.
May they honor these Lamas—
The highest of beings—
With endless showers of offerings.

May the lords of the sky
Send down the rains on time,
So to bring forth plentiful harvests.
May all existing governments
Make their decisions based on the teachings,
And thus may the whole world prosper.

May every medicine come to have
The power to cure; may the secret words
Fulfill all hopes.
May the minds
Of gods and spirits of sickness alike
Be overcome with thoughts of compassion.

May no single living being
Ever again feel a single pain.
May they never again feel afraid,
Never again be hurt by another,
Never again be unhappy.

May places of spiritual learning thrive,
Filled with people reading sacred books,
And singing them out loud as well.
May communities of spiritual practitioners
Live always in harmony, and may they achieve
The high goals for which they live together.

May all those who have ever taken
The vows of a monk come to master
The arts of solitude,
Throwing off every kind of distraction,
Gradually refining their minds,
Learning perfect meditation.

May nuns forever find support
For their physical needs, and live lives free
Of conflict or any outside threat.
May every person who's ever become
Ordained conduct themselves
Perfectly in their moral code.

And may any of those who may have ever
Broken this code regret what they have done,
And always work to clean the karma.
May they then return to a higher birth,
And in their new life never see
Their spiritual discipline fail again.

May every sage who lives in this world
Find the honor due to them,
and always be offered
The food and other needs they request.
May they always take care that
their hearts are pure,
And may they earn a good name that spreads
Throughout the entire world.

May none of these people ever again
Undergo the pain of the lower realms;
In strength beyond the strength of gods
May they quickly win the state
Of a fully Enlightened One
Without the slightest hardship.

May every suffering being there is
Make offerings over and over again
To every Enlightened Being there is.
And may the Enlightened Ones enjoy
Forever what we have offered them,
In infinite waves of bliss.

May every plan there is in the heart
Of every Bodhisattva to help
Every living being come true.
May everyone get every single thing
That the Enlightened Ones who shelter us
Have in mind for us to get.

May those who follow the lower paths
Of self-made awakened ones, and listeners,
Attain the happiness they seek.

And may we, through the kindness
Of Gentle Voice, remember in life after life
Who we are and what we practice,
Rejecting the worldly way of life
Again and again, until the day
We reach the level called Intense Joy.

May we gain the mystic ability
To live off even the poorest food,
Growing ever more strong and healthy.
In all our lives may we win the wealth
Of learning to live in solitude
With nothing more than barest needs.

And when anyone ever longs to see him,
Or ask him even the slightest question,
May the shroud which covers their eyes
Be torn away, so that the High Protector,
Lord Gentle Voice Himself,
Instantly appears.

We are working to achieve the goals
Of all the living things there are
In every corner of this universe;
And so by this power may we learn to do
Every single one of the things
That Gentle Voice is able to do.

And may we decide that we will stay
To work to clear away the pain
Of every living being there is
Until the last day of this
Universe; until the very last
Suffering creature is changed.

May every single pain that is coming
To any single being there is
Ripen now upon me instead.
May the great community of Bodhisattvas
Go forth and spread through all the world,
To work for the happiness of all.

The teachings of the Enlightened Ones
Are the one medicine that can cure
The great sickness of living kind.
They are the one ultimate source
Of every form of happiness.
And so by this power may the teachings remain
Long upon this planet, with all the support
They require, and all the respect they deserve.

And lastly do I bow myself
Down to the One with a Gentle Voice,
The One who has been kind enough
To teach me the ways of virtue;
Thus last do I bow myself down
To the One who was kind enough
To raise me up from childhood:
I bow to you
My Spiritual Guide.

*Guide to the Bodhisattva's Way of
Life* by Master Shantideva

INDEX

z

CPSIA information can be obtained
at www.ICGtesting.com
Printed in the USA
LVOW05s2249120716
496053LV00011BA/60/P